The Reluctant Detective Wants a Break

A Martin Hayden Mystery

by
Adrian Spalding

Contents

Preface 1
Chapter 1 7
Chapter 2 17
Chapter 3 26
Chapter 4 34
Chapter 5 42
Chapter 6 53
Chapter 7 64
Chapter 8 77
Chapter 9 87
Chapter 10 98
Chapter 11 110
Chapter 12 120
Chapter 13 136
Chapter 14 142
Chapter 15 165
Chapter 16 174
Chapter 17 188
Chapter 18 198
Chapter 19 206
Chapter 20 208
Chapter 21 212
Chapter 22 217
Chapter 23 222

Chapter 24	226
Chapter 25	230
Chapter 26	243
Chapter 27	252
Chapter 28	262
Chapter 29	265
Author Notes	274
Acknowledgements	276
Books by Adrian Spalding	277

The Reluctant Detective Wants a Break
Copyright © 2024 by Adrian Spalding.

All rights reserved. No part of this book may be reproduced in any form or by any electronic or mechanical means, including information storage and retrieval systems, without permission in writing from the author. The only exception is by a reviewer, who may quote short excerpts in a review.

This book is a work of fiction. Names, characters, places, and incidents either are products of the author's imagination or are used fictitiously. Any resemblance to actual persons, living or dead, events, or locales is entirely coincidental.

Preface

Harry proceeded exactly as instructed, driving on the very limit. Well, not his own limit, he could drive a good deal faster than this if he wanted to. In his own car, an elderly Vauxhall Corsa, with its customised wide alloy wheels, tinted windows and large bore deafening exhaust, he would be doing at least ninety miles an hour on any motorway. Today he was in the company car and as ordered he was sticking to the national speed limit, staying in the middle lane to let all those law-breaking, faster cars pass him with ease. At the same time, he could avoid the slow-moving lorries that trudged along the motorway, without the constant need to change lanes.

There had been a lot of debate to determine who should drive today. In normal circumstances Harry would have been automatically allocated the role. At only five feet tall, he was better suited to be the chauffeur. Not that he minded, he enjoyed driving, plus it was not as physically demanding as the other duties.

As soon as the team heard the request, two other designated drivers tried to convince the boss that they, and only they, could deliver on the unusual demand. There was a lot of discussion, not always that friendly. In the end, Barry, the owner of the company put his foot down; Harry was driving. Not that he was the best driver, it was because, he knew full well, putting him with the others would result in an unbalanced team. He wanted strength in his squad. Also, Harry was still young and relatively inexperienced, he had only been with the company two years; better for all that he remained the driver.

Smugly, Harry continued along the motorway making the most of it. The window opened just a crack, creating a howling sound that added to the excitement he felt coursing through his young veins. He would have opened the window fully to let the wind swirl around the vehicle as he maintained the legal speed limit, but his old grumpy partner, sitting in the passenger seat, complained that such a constant gust would give him a crick in the neck. For Harry, the old boy, even with his years of experience on the job, was a pain in the neck.

Yet in these unusual circumstances, there was still a certain standard to be expected. Driving carefully in the middle lane even at the national speed limit, cars and vans were still passing him, double taking at the rare sight on a motorway. He even noticed a couple of passengers leaning out their windows and videoing the spectacle on their phones. He posed with a look of importance just in case any of the recorded media went viral. How cool would that be? Him going viral across the internet would have to help the next time he attempted to pick up a girl.

Harry had never been successful on the girl front. It was either his height or his stammer, he was never sure which. No one told him it was his lazy eye, which led any potential partner to believe that he was not looking at them but checking out another female in the room.

"Hey Stirling Moss, don't forget it's the next turn-off," his colleague sounded cantankerous.

"I live not far from here; I know the road a lot better than you. Just relax, or am I driving too fast for you?" Harry laughed. He never stammered at work, only in the presence of an attractive woman.

He looked in his rear-view mirror. Taggart was following, just as he had been since they left the house, no doubt he was enjoying the experience as well. It wasn't his real name as that was some unpronounceable Scottish one, hence he was given the nickname, a lot easier for all concerned.

Harry signalled to move between two lorries as he prepared to turn off the motorway, he had plenty of time. It was at least another half a mile to the turn-off, he had no plans to brake heavily at the last moment, nothing so inappropriate for him. He wanted to prove to everyone that he was up to the task and could drive in a dignified way, demonstrating he was able to suppress the excitement of the mission.

To be fair to young Harry, it was not his fault. The subsequent police investigation showed beyond a shadow of a doubt the fault lay with the white van driver. A builder from Erith, having been bemused by the whole spectacle and not wishing to miss a moment, had leaned forward to continue observing in his cracked passenger door mirror. Distracted and not watching his direction of travel allowed his van to veer, hitting the metal central reservation. Well, not so much hitting, more scraping, not much damage, just an alarming sound that echoed throughout the van. The builder panicked.

This garnered an instinctive reaction from him. He swung the steering wheel left abruptly, away from the central barrier, which took his van into lane two, hitting at an angle of exactly sixty-three degrees, the side of Harry's vehicle. Having just indicated, Harry could not understand why he appeared to be spinning around traversing the motorway and heading for the hard shoulder. His automobile was taking a direction and speed that even with his foot pressed firmly on the brake pedal, or what he thought was the brake pedal in an act of innate panic, did little to stop the errant black Ford. It was only as he appeared to be still driving fast that he realised his error. He slammed his foot on the brake or tried to, but missing it completely the vehicle continued unabated.

By some quirk of fate, there was a field ditch which bordered the hard shoulder. Harry's vehicle struck the ditch, flipped onto its side and rolled twice, breaking through the wooden fence and finally coming to a stop right-side up in a field of maize. Harry had seen such spectacular accidents in the cinema, but this was his first. He was surprised just how much like the films the whole crash had been, noise, movements, breaking glass showering over him, before coming to a stop. The silence was deafening, something he always thought stupid, but now he understood.

Taggart watched in horror as Harry lost all control of the shiny black Ford which he had spent well over an hour cleaning in the morning. Helplessly he saw it veer across the motorway flip over and end up in a field. Well, he told them this morning, young Harry was not the best person to drive, now he'd been proved right.

If that was not bad enough, as the shiny black Ford clipped the ditch, the rear door burst open, allowing the loose contents to be thrown onto the motorway. A large white wreath with the word Hubby made up of flowers, instantly broke up on impact with the tarmac, leaving random letters scattered on the road.

Things got worse. Taggart watched in horror as the coffin broke loose, slid from its mountings and joined the other debris on the hard shoulder, the momentum making it roll awkwardly along the litter-strewn tarmac. The lid, which had been screwed on tightly, splintered before shattering along one side. Such was the catastrophic failure of the casket, the brown-suited body was ejected unceremoniously into lane one, where a Spanish articulated lorry swerved to avoid it. Luckily, the vehicle managed to evade the corpse, it would have been so unfair for anyone to die twice.

Taggart let out a strong expletive. Fortunately for the widow and her best friend in the back, his strong Glaswegian accent obscured the profanity. Not that either of his passengers would have heard it as both women were screaming.

Sensibly, so Taggart thought, he parked his limousine to act as a barrier to protect the body from other vehicles, which were either slowing or stopping to video as much as they could of this extraordinary traffic accident, all hopeful to make the early evening news. What Taggart with his best intentions failed to deduce was, the widow and her friend now had a grandstand view of the brown-suited inert body as it lay in the road looking up to heaven, maybe thinking, how on earth do I get up there?

The widow Christine was no longer screaming, even so her eyes remained firmly closed. As Sharon did her best to comfort her friend the thought of what happens next popped into her mind. Do we need another date for a funeral? Is there a backup coffin and hearse? Or even a nationwide recovery service for crashed hearses, although she thought that sounded like a poor business plan. In the end, do they all arrive at the crematorium late and have to wait until they can be fitted in? She was now in uncharted territory. Sharon looked down at the body through the door window. She looked at the eyes, the nose, the grazed forehead, the whole corpse. She looked again to be sure.

"Chrissy," Sharon tried to frame her words sympathetically, "you must look, that's not your husband. That's definitely not Alan's body."

Christine opened her tear-filled eyes, leant across Sharon and peered out of the window at the corpse.

"Jesus, what have they done with Alan?"

Chapter 1

The Papillon restaurant held many wonderful memories for Susan. It was the first posh place that Martin had ever taken her, to prove that he did not think her common. She almost blew the event thinking the restaurant was a themed diner for the film featuring Steve McQueen and Dustin Hoffman. That evening she learnt that it was in fact the French word for butterfly.

Then there was the time when he took her to The Papillon to say thank you for helping him during his mother's illness. Soon after that, he brought her to a discreet table in the corner of the restaurant to push a small box across the table containing a diamond engagement ring. Somehow, he had worked out her ring size and it fitted perfectly. That was such a fantastic memory only tainted by her scream, followed by a clumsy lurch at Martin to hug him, a movement during which she managed to knock over a bottle of chardonnay that hit the floor, bouncing twice before breaking. Apart from that it was a successful romantic meal.

They also came here the night they arrived back from their Italian honeymoon. They drank champagne and Susan sampled caviar for the first time. To her it was just an expensive version of the herring roe her dad bought from the fishmongers, although he drank Guinness with that, not champagne.

Since then, they had visited the place at least five maybe six times, occasionally with Martin's friends and once with her dad, who thought the whole place was overpriced and poncy. An opinion he didn't openly share with Martin but did with his daughter who he was proud of, as long as she remembered her Tooting roots.

"Mrs Hayden, your table is ready."

She was known to most of the staff, if not by name, by sight. It amused her to think that she could be regarded as a regular in this exclusive, expensive restaurant in the city. She followed the maître d' to the same small table where Martin had proposed. To her, it was almost like being at home wearing a pair of comfortable slippers.

She settled onto her chair. The attentive waiter beside her opened her napkin, placed it carefully on her lap and asked, "Would madam like to order a drink now, or await your guest?"

"No point wasting valuable drinking time, is there? Large chardonnay and a bowl of those nibble things please, can't be drinking on an empty stomach."

If Martin could have heard her, he would have laughed, saying, 'You can take the girl out of Tooting, but can't take Tooting out of the girl.'

Courteously the waiter nodded and retired to fulfil her request, leaving Susan to glance at the menu. She needed no more than a glimpse, she usually had the same dish. Lamb chops, although they were described more poetically, Susan knew they were still simple good old- fashioned lamb chops, almost as good as her mother used to cook.

Today she was waiting for a man, just not her husband. That still seemed an odd phrase, 'her husband'. But it was true, Martin had asked for a date when they were in Grantham. At first, she was lost for words, an odd experience for her, but she regained her composure quickly enough and thought it a good idea. In just three weeks, Martin had proposed. Swiftly he made all the arrangements to be married within four months of that first date. Now, only six months after their wedding, she was meeting, unbeknown to Martin, another man for lunch. Her mum would be turning in her grave, but in Susan's defence, she would point out it was purely business. It was just that Martin, as sweet as he was, still preferred to avoid too much detecting, in fact, his penchant was for no detecting at all.

After her second glass of chardonnay and clearing the small dish of cheesy nibbles, Susan became aware of a man standing by her table. She looked up, the man smiled warmly, looking down at her from what seemed to be a great height.

"Mrs Hayden?"

"Who are you?"

"Artemis Anthony Ellison, we spoke on the phone," he sounded slightly out of breath and very formal. "May I?" he gestured towards the chair opposite and waited for her to answer. She looked slightly confused by the arrival of her guest. Even though she was not aware of it, most of the diners in the Papillon were puzzled by the entrance of Mr Ellison.

The contact had begun with a telephone call two days prior. Susan had been in the Tower Bridge office of Martin Hayden Investigations, their only office and one of the smallest in the multi-use building. A detective agency without clients needs very little space. Susan had been online ordering a new carpet for the spare room at their house, which they now planned to make into a home office to avoid the need to travel into London.

During the call, Artemis Ellison seemed surprised that she was now Mrs Hayden, having previously been informed that she was Susan Morris, a director of Hayden Investigations. He had introduced himself as an insurance investigator.

He said he had a problem with a current case and he would like to enlist Hayden Investigations to help solve it. Flattery was the easiest way to get around Susan, so she was happy to meet Artemis for lunch to discuss the matter further. She was not going to mention the meeting yet to her husband, as he would no doubt decline offering any assistance to anyone.

"I'm sorry I'm a little late," Artemis apologised, "parking can be such a chore. With hindsight I should have made use of the tube, but it can be so hot and stuffy." He was still standing respectfully waiting for Susan to indicate that he could sit at her table.

Susan had expected the man to be suited and have a neat shirt and tie, an executive type. After all he did work for an insurance company. Even jeans and a leather jacket with a polo shirt might have been acceptable to her image of an investigator. The other diners would also have been happier to welcome such a man into their restaurant.

Artemis with his soft voice, was six foot six tall and solidly built, with a rounded face displaying a warm smile, clean shaven, as was his head, totally bald. He was carrying a well-worn cotton tote bag with an Utrecht FC badge over his shoulder. Artemis wore a shapeless red t-shirt, exposing his firm biceps. His vibrantly patterned cargo shorts, (it was not the weather or place for shorts) looked a little baggy on him. Susan did notice and was impressed by his expensive trainers yet not so enamoured by the patterned socks that did not match.

He looked as if he had just come off the beach, not walked into a very pretentious diner. Even so he stood patiently beside Susan, who had now been joined by a waiter unsure if the man should be ejected into the street, or treated with respect as one of the occasional eccentrics they often came across in their line of work.

"Please sit down," Susan proffered as if she was royalty. He complied, a little flustered, still berating himself for being late, which Susan dismissed. She ordered drinks, another for her and just sparkling water for Artemis as he requested.

As soon as they had ordered: lamb chops for Susan, chicken risotto for Artemis, Susan was keen to get cracking onto what this investigation was all about. Artemis did not have the same sense of urgency, choosing first to overly explain a little more about himself and his reasons for wishing to speak to Hayden Investigations, as well as saying he was sorry to hear that Martin was under the weather and unable to join them.

Susan, as she told Artemis that little white lie, consoled herself with the fact that Martin was under the weather. She imagined him standing outside a Honda dealer, in the sunshine just like everyone else. Ever since the new Honda Civic had come out, he had been eager to have a look at one in the flesh. In the end it had worked well for her appointment with Artemis, plus Martin gave her the go ahead for a new kitchen. Not that she needed Martin's permission, but it was useful for him to think he was involved.

Artemis had worked with the local insurance broker in Grantham, after a house had burnt down in strange circumstances. Martin and Susan had solved the mystery and caught the perpetrator for which Artemis was grateful, even though he had not had the opportunity to speak to them while they were there.

"You must understand that, as an employee of a large insurance company, my main role as an investigator is to ensure that the company doesn't have to pay out on claims if they are avoidable. Most of the time it's just a matter of ensuring that when someone claims for some gigantic flat-screen TV that was allegedly taken in a burglary, they had actually owned one in the first place. You'd be surprised and saddened to learn that victims of such crimes consider it an opportunity to refurbish their homes with the latest technology.

"However, there are times when client circumstances aren't a simple black-and-white decision. There are other factors which complicate everything and occasionally there is a moral duty on behalf of the insurance company. A responsibility that overall, my employers tend to ignore in their pursuit of profit."

Susan nodded, not that she had really followed what Artemis was getting at, but he seemed a nice man, barring his dress sense. Maybe another drink would help. She ordered one from the waiter who gave her a funny look. He probably knew she was Martin's wife and wondered what the bloke, who looked like a rugby player, was doing eating with her.

"But what do you want us to investigate?" Susan persisted. It had little effect, Artemis did things in his own time.

"I'm often uncomfortable following instructions from my superiors, when I can see that their decisions have a negative impact on the client, some of whom are vulnerable and ill-placed to fight a big insurance company. I sense that Hayden Investigations has a far better moral compass to guide it, with money not being the overriding force driving your work."

With three large glasses of chardonnay already consumed and a fourth just ordered, Susan had a little trouble translating that last sentence. In the end, she just presumed that it was well meaning.

"You do want us to investigate someone or something?" Again, Susan tried to move the conversation forward, unsuccessfully. She slumped back in her chair and listened.

"I was recently given a life insurance case. At first it was very humdrum, a husband dies following a tragic accident in his workshop, electrocution. The paperwork is quickly progressed, as it should be, and the process of paying the widow was about to begin, just as the funeral was being held for her departed husband.

"There followed a tragic road accident involving the hearse, which under the request of the deceased husband's wishes was travelling along at seventy miles per hour. During the crash, the coffin was ejected from the rear and tumbled along the road, causing it to break open and dispense the body."

"Lucky he was dead then," Susan commented with a big smile.

"Yes indeed." Artemis sounded a little irritated. "But that wasn't the biggest problem, which was the body that ended up on the tarmac was not known to any of the mourners. The corpse didn't belong to the husband."

"No shit! The husband and wife turning you lot over for life insurance by faking his death. Cool."

"Please could you give me a chance to explain before you jump to conclusions."

Accepting the reprimand, Susan sat back and listened to Artemis. Calmly he explained the body was that of an unidentified man similar in age to the husband. The most obvious explanation was, as Susan had already pointed out, that the husband was faking his death.

Artemis launched an inquiry which confirmed there had not been a mix-up with the bodies. The husband, if he was dead, was now missing. Without any proof of his death, the insurance company was not planning to pay out, leaving the faux widow with little income and no husband.

"The widow is left in a kind of limbo. Not only has she lost her husband, emotionally distressing enough, but she's also having to contend with the possibility of selling her house. A home that she has made, and now through no fault of her own may lose."

To Susan this sounded like a crusade and if there was one thing Susan liked, it was putting right a wrong. Without the slightest hesitation she asked, "How exactly can we help?" Then she added, what Martin would have considered to be a very mature caveat, "Given that you are an investigator for a big insurance company, with loads of resources and stuff, what can we bring to the case?"

Artemis smiled, carefully placed his used cutlery on his empty plate. "That was a very good risotto, although given the price, I would have expected it to be served on a silver platter. Risotto, even the best, is still very inexpensive."

He sipped his sparkling water in a very precise manner, then still holding his glass, he answered Susan's question. "My dilemma is, if there's the faintest chance she's in fact in cahoots with her husband, then I need to know. But I don't want to question her into submission. How bad would it look, an insurance company interrogating a poor widow?

"If you visit the wife, ask a few questions, she will know that an outside detective agency is also on the case. In her mind, the insurance company are taking the possibility of fraud very seriously. She, of course will not know anything about your company, for all she knows you might be the investigators version of Wonder Woman. If she's in cahoots with her husband, then she might under stress, or maybe fearful of your abilities, make an error, or trip up. I sincerely hope she doesn't, because as I have said I think the husband is dead somewhere. That's the only logical answer to this conundrum."

Wonder Woman did seem to be an erroneous description of Susan's detecting skills, nevertheless she took it as a compliment, which Artemis had not envisioned it to be.

"To be clear, you mean we, Hayden Investigations, will be there to rack up the pressure on the widow to see if she breaks?"

"I wouldn't have used those exact words, they are more akin to a Hollywood crime film, but yes. If Mrs Hall knows she's not a true widow and her husband is secreted in some hotel room, then your questions might just create a chink in her armour which my company can exploit."

"But you think she's a genuine widow, so why try and prove otherwise?"

Artemis put down his glass, brought his hands together and slowly intertwined his fingers. As he had feared, he was going to have to explain in words of two syllables his reasoning. Although the Grantham insurance broker had sung the praises of Martin and Susan, everything that Artemis had learnt about Hayden Investigations so far, had led him to believe they were a very amateur outfit.

"Should she be complicit in a fraud along with her husband, then they will both be facing a prison sentence. It will then become a police matter. As they say, if the stick bends and breaks it's no longer a stick. If it bends and remains a stick, it's true to itself."

Susan emptied her glass of wine, hoping to understand the meaning of that phrase. It made no sense even with the additional alcohol. She thought it best just to ignore it and move on.

"Okay, let me have her address and we'll pop round and have a word, put the screws on her."

"Thank you. Oh, there's one more small snippet of information that might help, although it might mean a visit to another address."

"Not a problem," Susan foolishly agreed, without asking for a little more detail.

Chapter 2

Martin was already beginning to regret the conclusion he had come to in haste and on the spur of the moment. To be honest the bottle of wine he had consumed did nothing to help his decision-making process. Even though Susan thought it a good idea as well, she had drunk a lot more than he had, so her judgement was equally impaired.

On paper, that is the estate agent's pamphlet, it did look a good idea. Moving away from Mother into a house of their own. A smart five-bedroomed house, not that Martin was planning children, more he was thinking of weekend guests. It was in a very sought-after part of Kent, Highfield. A detached, double garage, landscaped garden, although Martin had no interest in gardens, landscaped or otherwise. Yes, this was going to be the ideal location for them to begin their married life.

In Martin's alcohol-addled mind, he did not comprehend that Highfield in Kent is not and never will be on the London underground map. Also, the part of the village where their house was located comprised of little more than residential homes, unless you counted the post box and bus stop. If you wanted a shop, then a short drive to Highfield High Street was required. If that was not bad enough, Highfield was totally deficient in quality restaurants. What it did have was not anything special: a franchised pub, an odd-looking Italian restaurant that served beef burgers, and a grotesquely decorated Indian restaurant that bragged about a menu that fused Asian and American cuisine. Was that even possible? He doubted it.

Martin was missing the hustle and bustle of central London with its readily available cabs, underground trains and the wealth of well-appointed restaurants which understood their clientele.

As much as he wanted to spoil Susan with his announcement, the two of them still ended up in the back of an Uber, to be dropped off at a pub whose lacklustre menu had been decided upon by a group of dull executives, in an equally boring office block in Milton Keynes.

Soon after moving into their new house, Susan suggested upgrading the kitchen, as it had not been touched by the previous occupants in years. Martin was happy to let her sort that one out, talking to and liaising with builders was not his forte. New cars were to be his remit in this marriage. Susan knew what she wanted; all he needed was a microwave and a couple of gas rings, oh, and a kettle to be plugged in somewhere.

She quickly set about 'Project Worktop' as she liked to call it, with an enthusiastic vigour that impressed Martin. Each night she bombarded him with plans, estimates, colour samples and brochures, most of which he either nodded at or agreed were a good idea.

One breakfast, Susan proclaimed that she was going to accept an estimate from a builder, Baxter's Building Company. Odd initials, Martin thought, but if Susan was happy, so was he. They had given a date for when the work could commence and planned to have it completed within three weeks at the most.

During this discussion it occurred to Martin that at the time of the construction, the kitchen would be pretty much off-limits, as it would be for the most part in pieces. This led him towards the realisation that for three weeks they would need to live off the fruits of the local restaurants. That did not appeal to him. He had another idea, which he considered to be a stroke of genius.

"I have a surprise for you," Martin admitted, as the bored-looking waitress served his Hunter's Chicken Schnitzel. Not so much served, it was more throwing the plate down in front of him. Susan was shown the same level of indifference with her Beef and Chianti Casserole.

"I've got one for you too, but you go first," Susan agreed as she began eating.

"Well, as we have Baxter and company coming soon to knock out our kitchen, I was thinking of ways to circumnavigate the lack of cooking facilities in the house. Also, we've been married now for six months, and I know it is not a traditional anniversary, but I wanted to mark the occasion. Recalling what a wonderful time we had on our honeymoon, I thought it would be great to go back to Italy to see Verona, which we missed out on. I know you're not a great fan of Shakespeare, but two of his plays were centred there. You will be accustomed to Romeo and Juliet, and in Verona we can see Juliet's balcony."

As Susan pulled a sliver of beef from between her teeth, she asked, "Her balcony? I thought they were made-up characters in Shakespeare's warped mind."

"Far from it. The story is based on the lives of two real lovers who lived and died for each other in Verona in 1303. Shakespeare is known to have discovered this story in Arthur Brooke's 1562 poem of the tragic history of Romeo and Juliet. You and I will be able to see the actual balcony where she called out for her Romeo."

Martin looked smug as he continued, "I've booked flights and a little hotel just outside of the centre of the town. Three weeks for us to wallow in fine wines, superb cuisine, and bask in the history of a famous Italian town. Plus, we would avoid the builder's dust and the chaos at home."

Now as much as Susan was up for a few weeks of wine and top-class food, she was unsure how her own news might dovetail into Martin's plans. She had after all this afternoon, as a director of Hayden Investigations, agreed to look into the case of the missing body. Her problem was just how excited Martin looked at the thought of going away with his new wife. But a promise is a promise, or at least she should obtain all the facts first.

"Great! When are we going?" Part of Susan hoped that he was going to say in two months, even later in the year would have been a good thing, but having heard he was avoiding the builders, her expectations were low.

"Two weeks tomorrow we fly out, it fits in with the kitchen fitters' arrival," Martin boasted.

Not what Susan wanted to hear. To pour still more fuel on her predicament, he pulled two airline tickets from his pocket and waved them at her. "Do they actually do real paper tickets anymore? I thought everything was digital nowadays," she exclaimed.

"Not if you ask nicely and pay a little extra."

Martin was pleased with himself; Susan could see that. What she couldn't see was how to let him down gently given her earlier promise to Artemis.

With a serious look, Susan put down her knife and fork and leaned towards Martin, who at once realised something was amiss.

"Now don't get mad, Martin, but you know I mentioned earlier I had a surprise for you, well, it's nowhere near as exciting as flying off to Verona, few things would be. I mean treading in the steps of Shakespeare, phew, heavy stuff."

"He never went to Verona," Martin corrected, then asked, "What have you done?" He put down his cutlery with a look of despair.

"I have agreed to help a poor widow who needs support and comfort in bringing closure upon a tragedy that has blighted her. Her husband died."

"Most widows have a dead husband, or are you just attempting to distract me?"

"It won't take long, just a couple of days to clear up a misunderstanding, that's all. Plenty of time to pack for Verona. Let me explain."

"Oh, please do, Susan. I am eager to hear what sort of foolhardiness you have dropped me into."

Susan, as best she could without making it sound too onerous, explained how a body was mislaid by an undertaker. Leaving a poor widow, without any financial aid or assistance. She needed the support of Hayden Investigations to find her husband's body.

"We need to speak to the widow to reassure her that we will be doing our best to help." Deliberately, at this early stage of letting Martin down, she omitted to mention that the husband and possibly the wife might be involved in a fraud.

"Susan, my sweet darling wife, as usual you are making little sense. If the widow got in touch with you, why do we need to visit her?"

"Ah, that's because it wasn't her who asked, it was the insurance investigator on the case. Apparently, we developed a reputation after solving that mystery in Grantham." Susan could not hide the smugness in her voice.

"Then why is the insurance investigator not investigating, given his job title I would have thought it right up his street."

"Politics, Martin, company politics. Finish your chicken thingy while I map things out for you. The insurance investigator, a man called Artemis, which let's be honest is an odd name, but each to their own. Anyway, he pointed out that as far as his company is concerned, they don't plan to pay out on the life policy of the dead man without his body. As they see it, the policy holder is still alive, just not contactable. Now the thing is, it's in their interest not to find the body, why would they? Once it turns up, they will have to pay out thousands of pounds.

"Yet Artemis, for all his weird name and dress sense, I was surprised he was even served, still, money speaks louder than loud shorts. Artemis has a streak of human compassion running through him. He can see the widow emotionally distraught and lacking her husband's wage packet. He wants to find the body, but his company will not let him. Hence, he has turned to us, knowing what generous, kind people we are and knowing we have a natural instinct to fight for the underdog," Susan concluded.

Having now finished his Hunter's Chicken Schnitzel, which no doubt had been created at some large corporate focus group before being rolled out across the many branded pubs, Martin concluded that it must have lost a lot of flavour since that meeting, which was fortunate because it meant that Susan's enthusiasm to help a widow did not spoil it. The meal and the prospect of an investigation only helped to leave an uncomfortable taste in his mouth, which he washed away with a large glass of red wine before asking another simple question.

"This investigator, Artemis, you mentioned a weird dress sense. What are we talking about, poor colour coordination, old-fashioned jacket, baggy trousers?"

"Shorts and t-shirt, with one of those funny cotton type bags that environmentalists use. Mind, they come in handy."

"Shorts and t-shirt at the Papillon?

"Yep. Give the staff their due, they did tolerate him, I guess because you're so well-known there."

"Did he show you any form of identification: a business card, letter of authority or staff ID perhaps?"

"No, but he had a nice smile and was very pleasant."

"Are you sure he wasn't a mental case?"

The silence that ensued told Martin that the thought of Artemis being a fraudster had not crossed the excitable mind of his wife. He might well now be married to Susan, yet she was still the exact same person who had already led him into several scrapes.

"No way," she concluded, "if he was going to dupe me, he would have at least looked like an insurance investigator. I'm pretty sure he's legit."

"Pretty sure, that's reassuring. Okay, I'll be honest with you, I could spend the next twenty minutes arguing with you that we have no need to help anyone, let alone an eccentric insurance worker looking for a dead body. But I know, from bitter experience that such a debate would be futile. Hence to save time, I'll just ask what you have agreed to?"

"We're going to see the widow tomorrow, then we can judge for ourselves. See, I have changed, at least I negotiate better."

"Visit the widow, judge for ourselves?" Martin repeated. "I thought we were going to look for a dead body?"

"There's just a tiny, tiny chance that she might, in partnership with her husband, be attempting to defraud the insurance company. Us hard-nosed private eyes might just spook her enough if she's doing the dirty on the insurance company."

"Is there anything else you have not mentioned yet, which you might rely on, or want to investigate?"

"Funny you should mention that."

At this point, Susan confessed that Artemis had also asked her to speak to the funeral directors about the missing body. Her plan was to interview them, check their records and then she thought it should be easy enough to locate the missing body, leaving her plenty of time to shop and pack for Verona. She ended her explanation with a smile, which she hoped would soften Martin, generally that worked, not this time.

"Anything else?"

"Well, while we're at the undertakers, we do need to ask why they sacked someone so soon after the body went missing. Artemis thinks that odd, but that question is well outside his remit, but it could provide a clue that they did indeed mislay the body."

"Tell you what, Susan, I give up; I surrender. I do not want to hear another word. Let's get a cab, go home have a good night's sleep, and tomorrow you can tell me where you want to go, who you want to speak to, and I'll take you. That's what all good husbands do for their wives, so I am told."

Well, Susan thought, this marriage lark is working well.

Chapter 3

The presumed deceased Mr Hall and his probably widowed wife, lived in a fashionable part of town, smarter than Martin had imagined given Susan's description of a wife living in destitution.

The house was fully detached. Martin admired the Tudorbethan style, probably built around the 1930s. It was half-timbered with a mix of herringbone brickwork and a little pebbledash. The windows no longer had the original wooden frames with iron casements, although the modern double-glazing still had diamond-shaped panes, in tribute to the original.

The roof had red clay tiles and an elaborate chimney stack. It had an oak front door with iron nails and fittings. The Halls' residence had a two-storey bay window with half-round sides. All was very much an estate agent's dream.

A big garage on the left of the house looked to be a later addition. The brickwork, in Martin's opinion, was a poor match. He was not normally interested in the architecture of buildings, residential or otherwise. It was just that the house in front of him was a carbon copy of the one his mother grew up in. No doubt it was the same builder, just a different area to his mother's childhood surroundings.

As Susan rang the bell, she hoped Mrs Hall would be home. Last night she had inferred to Martin that all the arrangements had been made. They had not. Susan had been distracted by a documentary on popular cocktails. She let out a sigh of relief when the door opened.

The woman who opened the door stared suspiciously at the uninvited visitors. Her grey-green eyes looked up at Martin before flicking towards Susan. Mrs Christine Hall was short, a little over five feet, with rusty-blonde hair, a slender body and a face that looked younger than the thirty-three years she had lived. Still, it had a tired appearance to it and the laughter lines around her eyes had given way to a worried frown.

"Mrs Hall, this is Martin and I'm Susan, of Hayden Investigations. Artemis Ellison from the insurance company has asked us to talk to you, hopefully to resolve the unusual matters surrounding your husband's tragic death." Susan sounded sympathetic to the task at hand, which impressed Martin. She was more often blunt and to the point, today she sounded almost professional.

"I thought the insurance company had given up on finding my husband." Christine's voice was stern, almost hateful, she had had enough of people saying they were going to help, then doing nothing.

"The company has not exactly given up; it's just more appropriate if an outside contractor deals with the matter. May we come in?"

Martin could not help himself, he looked at Susan thinking she must have been taking evening classes on interview techniques without his knowledge.

They followed her into the living room at the front of the house, overlooking the tree-lined road visible through the net curtains that were draped around the bay window. A row of condolence cards, not as many as Martin had expected, were standing on the marble mantlepiece that was affixed over the faux coal fire waiting to be switched on.

Martin examined the space, the furnishings, the wallpaper, the oddments of bric-a-brac that littered the room. He hated the place. The bold flowery wallpaper would give him a migraine. It was lucky his new wife was happy with plain colours and content to organise the decoration of their new home with an uncluttered theme.

After they refused her offer of a drink, Mrs Hall sat down opposite her guests in a leather chair which Susan recognised as being from IKEA, having considered purchasing one for the spare bedroom.

"Comfortable?" Susan asked.

Christine looked a little confused at the question. "As good as can be expected, it hasn't been long since Alan died."

"Sorry, I should have made myself clear, the chair?" Susan pointed at where Christine was sitting, "The chair, is it comfortable? It felt okay in the shop, but unless you spend an hour or two on it, which is not possible in IKEA without looking as if you are squatting, you can't really tell how comfortable it's going to be."

"Oh, yes, it's fine, really comfortable," she replied, sounding a little confused and apprehensive.

Once Susan had received feedback about the chair, she looked at Mrs Hall, who now insisted on being called Christine.

"I'm getting one for the spare room, well, planning to. Decorating is such a bore."

'Ah well,' Martin thought, 'that's the professionalism all used up.' He interrupted his wife, "The insurance company has given us some details about your husband, but if we could hear from you a little more about how he died and the confusion that followed the unfortunate accident with the coffin. If it's not too painful for you," he added as a sign of empathy.

They already knew from Artemis's description that she had been married for ten years. Christine currently works as an admin clerk at a local plumbing and heating company. She was originally from Crawley, but now was living in Sidcup.

She spoke clearly, with just a hint of emotion in her voice. Martin was fully aware that she would have related this story to the police already, clearing up any uncertain memories, hence her recall was very precise. Maybe a little too precise, Susan thought.

When Alan, her husband, was found on the floor of his workshop, she was with a friend in Crawley. An old school friend whom she often popped in to see. She was staying there for three nights, helping with the garden, moving shrubs and replanting, to fit in with the new decking the family was having.

She was asleep, it was about two in the morning when Ian, Alan's best mate, called to say there had been an accident. Alan had died. She did not go straight home, there was no point. She stayed until the morning when her friend drove her back. She couldn't bear to stay at the empty house, so she grabbed a few things and stayed with another friend while the funeral arrangements were made. It wasn't until about three days later that she returned to the house and stayed the night. It was a hard, lonely night, she confessed.

She wiped a small tear from her eye with a tissue as she related the circumstances of the traffic accident and the body lying on the road. She hadn't looked at first, but her friend, Sharon, told her it was not Alan.

"But when you saw your husband in the Chapel of Rest, there was no mistaking it was him in the coffin?" Susan asked, recalling the time she had seen her mother laid out serenely after her cycle accident.

"I never saw him in the coffin, or at any time after his death," she admitted, surprising Susan and Martin, who had assumed that she would have had one last look at her husband after he died so suddenly. "It's a quirk, I assure you, nothing sinister. I saw my mother in a Chapel of Rest and that's the first image I have whenever I think about her. I didn't want that to happen with Alan. I have always said, I would never gaze upon him once he died. I want my lasting memory to be him alive, smiling and talking. People think I'm mad, but that's just the way I am."

She agreed when asked, that the last person to see Alan was his best friend, Ian.

"To be honest, I can tell you Ian and some of Alan's work colleagues, have been really helpful during this difficult time. One of them even popped round to ask if I was going to bury Alan in his hi-vis vest. We did laugh. I know that must sound so irreverent to you, but it was the first time I had laughed since he'd died. Laughter does help. Anyway, I told him I was planning to have Alan buried in his favourite brown suit, the one I hated so much," she smiled. "I do miss him," she added with a melancholy tone.

Then she continued, maybe taking the opportunity to unburden herself with two strangers. She worked for a local company, not earning a great deal of money. Now with Alan gone and the insurance company not paying out, she was facing an economic catastrophe. There was the mortgage that she could no longer afford, and the bills, as well as buying clothes and food.

"Through no fault of my own, the undertaker's incompetence has left me in a position where unless they find Alan's body soon, I will need to sell the house and find somewhere to rent. The future was going to be bleak without my husband anyway; without his body, it looks dreadful."

Susan next wanted to touch on a question she knew might not be diplomatic, but she was not known for her diplomacy skills.

"Is it conceivable that your husband might have faked his death? He wouldn't be the first."

Christine smiled; it was an accusation that she had been asked about before. The insurance company had pressed her on it. She had guessed they would have looked closely at the relationship between her and her husband. They had found nothing. Christine answered Susan, "He doesn't have the intelligence for such a fraud, if he tried, he'd only screw it up.

"Are you aware that soon after the undertakers lost Alan, something they have repeatedly denied, they sacked one of their young workers. I heard that through the grapevine. Possibly they found the truth but were just not keen on sharing it. Bad for their image, I guess."

"Is it possible we could speak to Ian, the best friend?" Susan asked, producing a look of resignation from Martin.

"I'm sure he won't mind, I can give you his address. He's usually at home during the day as he drives a local taxi at night."

Martin asked a question that had been bugging him all the while he was sitting in Mrs Hall's lounge. "When your husband died, the funeral was held within a week, which seems very quick. I have heard of people having to wait more than a month to have their loved ones buried."

"Everything has been a bit of a whirlwind, plays havoc with the emotions. There was a cancellation, so they were able to slip Alan in. Looking back that was a bad choice."

Martin accepted the answer without asking for further clarification. He was unsure just how funeral directors might have a cancellation unless it was a very serious case of misdiagnosis.

"Well?" Martin asked as he followed Susan along the pristine flagstones that led away from Mrs Hall's house, back through the small wrought iron gate and onto the pavement. "Did we spook her, as you hoped we might do? Trick her into saying her husband is living the life of Riley somewhere?" There was a sign of mockery in his voice.

"Well, the house was a lot better than I imagined an airport worker's might be. But she was distraught, genuinely, I thought. Time to speak to the best friend."

"About that," Martin pointed out, "a new line of enquiry?"

"All good detectives start with the last person to see the victim alive. We're good detectives, trust me on that one, Martin. It's just that most investigations start with a dead body, with this one, finding the body will solve the whole thing."

Martin did not see the funny side of that as he drove away from the Hall residence, towards the address that Christine had given them.

Chapter 4

Ian Cook had been a thin man since a child. He could eat volumes of food, in the main unhealthy and fattening, none of which added a pound to his slender frame. Yet now aged thirty-five he was starting to develop a little extra girth on his waist, middle-age spread for Ian was coming early.

"So let me get this right, you're working for the insurance company, you're not the police or anything like that?" Ian asked as Martin shifted his chair slightly to get some shade from the large parasol that shielded the wooden garden table from the strong sunshine. Susan looked happy to lounge in the warmth of the sun's rays.

Martin could not help but make a mental note of the objects on the table. A large citronella candle that was alight, three empty San Miguel beer bottles, alongside the discarded cardboard packaging, with the fourth bottle in Ian's hand, from which he sipped from time to time. Also, there was a Burger King bag screwed up which very likely contained the debris from Ian's early takeaway lunch. That made Martin aware he was hungry. Not that he ever ate fast food, it was just he had eaten an early breakfast, as Susan had insisted on it.

"Not the police, only supporting the work of the insurance company. In the main, to either prove or disprove Mr Hall's current whereabouts."

"Detectives, a bit like Starsky and Hutch or Mulder and Scully. Yeah, she's a good looker, Scully, always fancied her. What about you two, getting it on?" Ian suggested with a grin.

"More like Shaggy and Scooby-Doo," Martin suggested before Susan added, "Well, I do sleep with him every night, it's the way he pays me. Not a bad deal."

Martin felt himself blush as Ian looked a little confused, her answer hadn't sounded like a joke.

"Anyway, is he dead or is he alive? Alan Hall?" Martin asked, changing the subject, as he noticed Susan had closed her eyes and was no doubt imagining herself on a Spanish beach, after embarrassing the men around her.

"He's dead, one hundred per cent. I saw him on the floor. Christ! it was a shock." There were a lot of questions that Martin wanted to ask. He hoped they would soon be answered as Ian automatically recalled that night.

Ian Cook and Alan Hall had been working at the airfield, Potts Fields. Working nights, when the airfield was closed, they used the time repairing equipment, upgrading lighting. There were always several jobs they took on under the general heading of maintenance. They never worked on the aeroplanes, which requires specialised skills, for which they were not qualified, Ian pointed out.

It was just after midnight, they had finished most of the tasks they had been allocated, and now they were kicking their heels a little.

"It was then Alan started talking about this new laser self-levelling kit he had bought, reckoned it was the business. I was interested, it sounded pretty cool and suggested he bring it in the next night. But he goes one better and says, 'Let's pop back now, I'll give you a demo and then we'll be back well before anyone turns up.' 'Why not,' I said, he was, after all, my boss being the senior bloke.

"We get back to his house. Both of us go in and then out into his workshop. He starts unpacking this DeWalt box with the leveller in. I go off to get a couple of beers from the fridge. When I come back, he's on the floor, face down. Having been trained in first aid and stuff I knew not to touch the body. I checked for electrics, well, I saw the wire, went over to the wall, pulled the plug out and then tried to help him. He wasn't breathing or anything, so I called the ambulance. Christ, it seemed like forever before they came.

"They tried to revive him with that paddle thing they have, but none of it helped. He was dead." Ian stopped to take a long gulp from his beer before continuing,

"Now they've lost him. Christ, he could be anywhere, stuck in a fridge someplace, no one knowing who he is. The funeral people have made a right pig's ear of this."

"Paddle thing? Do you mean a defibrillator?" Martin queried, to be sure the emergency services were not beating the body with a canoe paddle.

"That's the one," Ian confirmed.

"Two things." Susan asked, "One, what was he doing holding onto a live wire? And two, shouldn't the RCD fuse, now standard in domestic settings, have cut the power the moment Alan touched the wire?"

Martin and Ian looked at Susan, who still had her eyes closed.

Ian sat up in his chair; he looked surprised to have been asked such questions about that night. Martin was still more astonished that: one, Susan was paying attention and two, she knew what an RCD fuse was.

"I have no idea what he was doing with a live wire in his hand. I can't even speculate. As for the fuse, Alan's a naughty boy, his whole workshop bypasses the domestic fuse box and the meter, free electric. He always likes to get what he could on the cheap."

It was a small insignificant sign, Martin thought. 'Alan's a naughty boy', was that Ian tripping himself up knowing Alan is still in the land of the living, or was it just a turn of phrase with him not yet used to his friend having passed away. Martin was unsure. Either way he made no comment. He wanted to know a little more about why Ian and Alan were working together after Christine had mentioned Ian was a night cab driver.

There was another surprise from Ian's reply. It turned out that he was only working alongside Alan as a temporary arrangement, with Alan paying him cash in hand to help him on nights. Normally, Alan worked with another man, a correctly employed man, but he had damaged his knee in a motorbike accident.

Alan needed to find a replacement fast, so asked Ian to step in. After he died, Ian could not go back to the airfield. Now the bloke with the injured knee was back and they had employed a replacement for Alan fast, which Ian thought inconsiderate.

"Tell me, why was it up to Alan to find cover for an employee off sick?" Martin asked as Susan seemed to have zoned out again.

"I think it was more they wanted someone trustworthy and honest, who was immediately available. Well, it was an airport of sorts. Alan told them I'm reliable and honest, hence, I got the gig."

If Martin was not a professional, he would have burst out laughing. Potts Field might be an airfield, but it certainly was not an airport. He knew of the place, no more than a big field in which prosperous old men flew in and out of to show off their expensive toys.

"How was Alan's and Christine's relationship, all happy?"

"Yeah, I think so, as much as anyone can see. They appeared to be a happy couple, the odd cross word, but which married couple doesn't have a bit of a barney once in a while."

"How long have you known Alan?"

"Worked together years ago installing air conditioning ducts in new builds. Just seemed to hit it off and we've been pals ever since. Try to catch up once a week for a beer or two."

"Has he had any affairs?"

"What Alan? Nah, straight as a die."

"Not even a sly glance at a pretty girl?"

"Not Alan."

Susan, her eyes closed, was listening. In the past she had often heard men making excuses. She had found, that when you were asking questions, the shorter the responses were, the more likely there was a lie hiding behind it. Almost as if the person being questioned had decided the less said, the lower the chance of being found out.

Ian's answers had gone from the detailed and embellished, to a simple 'Not Alan'. Susan was suspicious.

"Working nights with Alan doesn't leave much time for a day job. Do you have regular employment?" Susan had now opened her eyes and wanted him to tell her what his actual job was, to see whether he confirmed what Christine Hall had said.

"Mini cab driver, well Uber to be precise, allows me to pretty much please myself, choose my own hours and not have a boss breathing over my shoulder. The gig with Alan was a handy regular bit of cash income. Got the car on contract hire so need to keep the cash coming in."

A long answer, Susan thought.

Since the moment she had listened to Artemis, Susan had a question. Well, she had more than one, but there was a certain issue she was dying to ask about. It was one of those problems that you know full well will upset the person you question. It will create a reaction. Now she was going to get the chance to raise it.

"If it wasn't Alan Hall lying dead on the floor, who was it?" Susan waited, knowing full well that Ian having drunk four bottles of San Miguel was not going to take kindly to what she was alleging.

"What sort of stupid bloody question is that? I saw Alan, my best mate, on the floor dead. It's not something you mistake or forget. Speak to the ambulance blokes, the undertaker's van that took him away, it was Alan, they just lost him somewhere. They're the ones you need to talk to."

Susan was not convinced, some men lie, and some of those who do have a hard time covering their untruths.

"But suppose the audit trail from the workshop to the broken coffin on the trunk road shows, without a doubt, that it was the same body that was picked up from the workshop. In that case you are either wildly mistaken or lying."

"Alan Hall is dead, I saw him. I tried to revive him, and he's dead, that's the fact. You need to look at the undertakers again lady. If you want my opinion, Alan has been cremated under another name."

"You tried to revive him, you didn't mention that earlier, you just said you called the ambulance."

Ian finished his last bottle, slammed it down on the table, causing the empty Burger King bags to jump up. He turned to the duo with a menacing look. That did not worry Susan in the least, the weedy Ian might try and throw a punch, but she assumed Martin would protect her, or vice versa.

"I shook him a few times, he didn't respond."

"Was that the extent of your first aid training?"

"You're a right smart arse. Alright I shit myself, my best mate was lying dead on the bloody floor. I panicked, I couldn't do anything, I was helpless. I just did the three nines and hoped they would be in time. They were not. That night is my worst nightmare. Just find him for me, I know he's dead, please find him."

Susan recalled sitting in Le Papillon listening to Artemis asking for help. Back then it had sounded a simple task. A mislaid body. It sounded easy, possibly even straightforward. The body had to be somewhere. A clerical error would have been her best guess. That was until she listened to Ian Cook.

If there was one thing Susan had over Martin, it was she had a lot of experience with men. Mostly unreliable ones, who would arrive home stinking of alcohol and categorically deny they had been drinking. This had given Susan the ability to tell if a man was lying, and Ian Cook was unquestionably lying.

That was not a big deal. They were still looking for a mislaid body. It was the circumstances surrounding that body that now began to dawn on Susan.

Ian was lying. Therefore, Alan was alive somewhere, maybe hiding from his wife, possibly living with a new wife. But Alan was not on the floor of the workshop when Ian called the ambulance. The burning question was, who was dead on the floor? And more worrying where did Ian and Alan get the body from? Suddenly Susan regretted smiling at Artemis and saying, 'Of course, we'd love to help.'

Chapter 5

"You look nothing like a private detective," was the comment Barry Gladstone, of Gladstone Funeral Directors - established 1984 - made as Susan sat down in front of him.

"Gladstone sounds nothing like a funeral parlour to me. These things are the irony of life," she responded.

Barry had to agree that the business his father started, could very well have been called anything other than the family name of Gladstone. It was something that had always haunted him. Even Headstone might have been better, but his father thought he knew best and until he finally became a customer, the name would have to stay.

Barry looked at his latest visitor who introduced herself as a partner of a detective agency he had never heard of called Hayden Investigations. Barry hoped this was not going to be a sort of confidence trick. Was she from the newspapers trying to get another angle on the story that had given him nightmares over the past weeks?

For her part, Susan thought the office of Barry Gladstone could have done with a good spring clean. Starting with the deep-pile carpet which looked as if it had been supplied by Cyril Lord back in the sixties and had not been cleaned since the day it was laid. The whole office could have been designed and furnished in the nineteen-fifties. Susan wondered if being an undertaker made you mundane in the design and sparse in the hygiene departments, after all, the clients who resided temporarily in the on-site fridges would never complain.

She would have hoped to be sitting in front of Barry Gladstone with Martin beside her. That hope had fallen apart as they parked outside the undertakers in one of the many empty customers' parking spaces.

"I'm not going in," Martin abruptly declared.

"Why?" Susan made a questioning look.

"We might see a dead body and I don't want to see one."

"They don't have examples of their work in the reception area, you're not going to see a dead body."

"There might be one being pushed around."

"Don't be so stupid, Martin, why would they have a dead body hanging around? I know you saw your father after his death."

"That was completely different, he was my father, I knew him. It is not the same to view a dead stranger, which is wrong and a little unsettling."

Martin was adamant he was not going to budge, that was clear. Without another word, Susan exited the car, slammed the door and walked into the undertakers.

It was not often that funeral directors lost bodies. The occurrence is thankfully rare. That was why Susan, after a little research, had found a great number of column inches in newspapers dedicated to the negligence of Gladstone's. Susan guessed that the company would be fed up with such questions. Her arrival, on behalf of the grieving widow, assuming she was one, would do nothing to endear her to the company. But, if she appeared to be on the side of the dismissed worker that Mrs Hall and Artemis mentioned, then maybe she stood a chance of getting her foot in the door and in front of someone important. Fortunately, Mrs Hall had known the name of the sacked employee.

"I'm here on behalf of Ashe Hurst, the worker I understand you dismissed recently for, as he puts it, losing a body. I want to see if there is any way we can help you reconsider before the poor boy, unable to pay his rent, ends up homeless. I'm sure he never meant to lose any of your deceased customers."

"You are asking me to discuss a matter that's confidential between employer and employee. I can't agree to that without Mr Hurst being present."

"Well, it's not exactly a state secret that you did lose a body, after your drag racing driver sent a coffin crashing along the motorway, discharging its contents onto a busy trunk road. I'm just here to ensure that Ashe isn't the scapegoat for your cock-up."

"It wasn't a cock-up." The retort was immediate and sharp from Barry, who had had enough of the press interviews, the allegations and the innuendos after the unfortunate incident. Not only had he had to endure police digging around all his files and records, but the press was also more than excited that a body had fallen out of a coffin onto the road. If that was not bad enough for Gladstone Funeral Directors, the body that ended up on the tarmac was not the one that should have been inside the coffin in the first place. To make things still worse, the National Association of Funeral Directors had got themselves involved and peeved Barry as he was hoping to be voted in as their next president. That dream had soon gone up in a puff of smoke when that bloody body bounced along the trunk road.

"The police and other authorities have been assured that the body we picked up and was at that time identified as Alan Hall, was the same physical body that was unfortunately involved in a road traffic accident. The circumstances regarding the misidentification of the body is not due to any errors made by Gladstone Funeral Directors."

"Then why sack the guy if he never lost a body?"

"As I said, that's a matter between ourselves and Mr Hurst, even if your detective agency is working on his behalf." Which of course it was not, it was just the impression that Susan had successfully given to Barry.

"Why waste your time and mine, insisting that I go back to our offices, drag Ashe Hurst down here, so he can sit next to me while you try and justify sacking him for losing a body that was according to you never lost in the first place?" Susan held her breath, seeing if the bluff worked.

This was the part that Barry hated about being an owner of a company, people brought you anguish. He had no objections to the grief that associated itself with death, which was his business after all. It was the pain of dealing with problems, he hated confrontations. His father loved arguing, shouting and generally annoying people, it was Mr Gladstone senior's forte. Old man Gladstone would happily spend all day with you arguing that the Earth was flat, even though he knew it to be round. Barry was nothing like his dad. He enjoyed tending to the deceased, ensuring they looked their best for the final time their relatives were to see them. He liked dressing up in his garb and walking in front of the hearse. It made him feel good to show honour and respect to the departed. He also hoped that same respect made those left behind feel better as they watched their loved one slip behind a curtain to be burnt to ashes.

Conflict was not Barry's strong point. This female investigator had a point, it would not take much for her to bring Ashe back to the office and that would have made things worse. At least with Ashe absent from the room, he could speak his mind without fear of being taken to some employment tribunal.

"He wasn't sacked for losing a body," Barry admitted. "Before I tell you the real reason, you need to promise me that you will not share the information outside of this room."

If there was something that Susan treasured above most things, it was a secret. She loved knowing one, it gave her a feeling of power. Not that she was any good at keeping them. She was the worst person in the world that you would want to give one to.

"Cross my heart," Susan answered, knowing full well that she would be telling Martin the moment she got back in the car. How bad could it be? It was grimmer than even Susan had imagined.

Visibly jittery, Barry explained. During the police investigation into the misidentified body, Barry had spoken to each member of staff who had come anywhere near the supposed corpse of Alan Hall. To provide himself with an accurate list, Barry had checked the entry and access records for the mortuary area on the premises. An area restricted and only accessible by a smart pass which Barry had introduced three years ago. It was by most standards a little over the top, body snatching was no longer a popular crime in modern-day England. He had bought the system more out of impressing the female representative selling the product than any real need to have it installed.

During his reviewing the entries and exits he noticed one of his employees, Ashe Hurst, entered the building late at night on several occasions. He would spend the best part of an hour inside before leaving. Odd behaviour which Barry, as much as he would have liked to, could not ignore.

When confronted with the evidence Ashe was more than surprised that his nocturnal visits to his place of work had been uncovered. He offered several implausible reasons for being there. It was only when Barry threatened to give the information to the police, in case it helped the investigation, that Ashe admitted his motive.

"You're telling me," Susan stated, to make sure she had heard correctly, "that sweet little Ashe," another assumption, which in the light of the revelation was way off the mark, "was taking pictures of dead bodies and then posting them on a website. I'm shocked there's even one for that sort of thing."

"I think you'll find there's a website for just about any depravation you can imagine. I couldn't have him on the premises a moment longer, but I couldn't risk that sort of scandal surfacing. So, I gave him a good redundancy payment and told him we'll connect his dismissal to the wrongly identified body."

"Well, serves him right."

"I presume you'll be telling your client he has no case?"

"My client? Oh Ashe, of course, he's history now I can tell you. But what about Mrs Hall, a widow who might not be a certified widow until she finds the body of her husband. Where does she stand in all this mess do you think?"

Barry shrugged. He had not thought about her since he tried to get her to pay for the funeral she had ordered. She pointed out, when Barry presented his final account to her, that the body was not that of her husband so why should she pay? That might be so, Barry argued delicately, but she had ordered it in good faith. That had gone down like a lead balloon. Luckily for Barry he found out that his business insurance covered him for such losses and so he eagerly claimed as much as he could. Plus, as a bonus, he still had the unidentified body under his care, so someone somewhere was going to pay a fortune in storage costs. Every cloud and all that, assuming the body was finally identified. Mrs Hall did not concern him anymore.

"Out of my hands."

"Yes, you told me," Susan replied with a weary tone. "The body was misidentified, and you were in the clear. But Mrs Hall, she now has no husband and no insurance pay-out until they find him. How does that work?"

"I don't really care, that's down to the insurance company, who between you and me suspect that Mr Hall might well have faked his own death. Not unheard of you know."

'Between you and me' sounded as though the barriers that Barry had put up earlier had now been taken down. It was after all a well-known news story, so why not find out some of the behind the story details?

"Then why was your man tearing down the motorway like a racing driver?"

"Mr Hall had made a range of odd requests in the event of his death."

Susan knew there was the now infamous desire for the hearse carrying his body to travel along the A2 at the legal limit of seventy miles per hour – Mr Hall liked speed.

"Apart from the speeding thing what other out of the ordinary wants from the Hall family did you get?"

Barry paused, no doubt recalling the order in his mind. He rattled off, like the true professional he was, the coffin type, only one car in addition to the hearse, flowers to be sent to the house and collected from there. Just two people in the car following the hearse, which now everyone knew was to be driven at seventy miles per hour. There had been four private cars following the entourage, just friends. Simple humanitarian service as Mr Hall was not religious. Cremation required, no burial. They chose the suit he had to be buried in and a set of tools was placed in the coffin.

"Entry song: 'All by myself', interval song: 'God shuffled his feet', exit song: 'Another one bites the dust'. The following day we were to collect the flowers and take them to a care home, but that never happened for obvious reasons." Barry sighed, his corporate brain was still working on what he could have charged, thank God for insurance.

"The originals?"

"What?" Barry was unsure of what the question referred to.

"Eric Carmen, Crash Test Dummies, Queen."

"Oh, the songs, yes, easy nowadays with Spotify. Very old school, wouldn't have thought they were your type of musical genre?"

"Hold on," Susan interrupted, ignoring Barry's remark, "a set of tools in the coffin? Are we talking Black and Decker workstation, pneumatic drill?"

"No, a simple set of lock picks. It would seem the weird Mr Hall had a fear of being buried alive, so he wanted some tools so he could get out. Not that they would help, it's not as if we use a Yale lock on the coffin; we screw the damn thing down tight."

"Not tight enough, it would seem." Susan could not help the jibe. "Any other odd requests while we're on the subject?"

"No, that was the limit for him. There are very few traditional cremations in these enlightened times. If I had my way, there would be none of these disrespectful songs, jokes and wacky modes of transport. Not forgetting the odd irreverent requests."

"But it pays the bills?"

"If we didn't do it, then someone else would."

"What happened to the tools?" Susan asked, noticing the office was getting warmer. Barry too was feeling the heat as he removed his tie, meticulously rolled it up and then popped it into one of his desk drawers.

"Never recovered after the accident. But they could have been thrown anywhere, we weren't bothered and the family have never mentioned them. Look, I know what you might be thinking, but rest assured, if he was alive in that coffin, those puny tools wouldn't have afforded his escape."

"And the unidentified body? What's happening about that?"

"We're hanging onto the John Doe until the police conclude their investigations, which I gather isn't any time soon."

Susan stood up preparing to leave the stuffy office, which was making her eyes feel heavy. Her mind was still pondering the circumstances of Alan Hall's death. It was his best friend who had called the ambulance upon discovering Alan on the floor of his workshop. She tried to picture the ambulance staff arriving, then seeing that Alan Hall was dead, calling the undertakers, who in turn took away the body.

"How do you identify the bodies when they arrive here, it's not as though they can talk."

"If they could, we'd throw them out for not being the correct clientele." Barry giggled at his humour before continuing, "A brown cardboard luggage label is tied on the wrist and another on the ankle. Name, date of birth if possible, pick-up location and a number, just in case we end up with two John Smiths. It means they can stay on until the cremation or burial. Very eco-friendly."

"But who gives you the name of the person?"

"In this case it was the ambulance staff, who, as I understand, received the information from the informant, Ian Cook, a colleague of the deceased, if he's deceased. Who can really know?"

***

"A brown tie-on label; are you joking?" Martin raised his eyebrows in wonder.

"No, I don't think you can get more old-style than a tie-on label. I'd have thought they would have bar codes or other fancy stuff, it's not as though funerals are cheap, is it?"

"Where to next, or have we now finished our investigation?" Martin asked, thankful they were at last moving away from the undertakers.

Chapter 6

"Why is it you never visit your father?" Caroline asked as she dried a cracked dinner plate before leaving it on the cluttered worktop. She had no idea where her brother stored his crockery, even if she had, it would have been wrong, her brother was that contrary.

"Why should I? He never visits me," Artemis answered, without looking up from the book he was reading: 'The Resurgence of Parish Council Powers in England', which he deemed to be a lot more interesting than listening to his whining sister.

"But he's your father, you should go and see him once in a while."

That was typical of his sister, he thought, instructions to be obeyed. Artemis would have preferred some logic applied, pointing out the reasons why he should visit his father. That was the way he liked to do things. Being told what to do was not the best approach for him. Something Caroline had yet to learn.

Artemis slid a bookmark over a page before closing his book. He resigned himself to not being able to concentrate while his sister was in one of her righteous moods. He looked across the kitchen to her as she folded the tea towel with a little too much precision for his liking.

"Charles the Third is my monarch, I never go and see him, because in much the same way, he and my father don't visit me. My father has never set foot in this house, I can't see why the onus should be mine and mine alone."

"You can be so impossible at times. At least we still keep in touch."

"Only because you invite yourself whenever it suits you and I can't find a reasonable pretext not to open the door to you."

Caroline joined him at the kitchen table. She was four years older than her brother and had always taken it upon herself to be his guide and protector. However unwelcome her efforts were, she persisted with her self-inflicted responsibilities.

They were almost born in West Yorkshire, equally they were almost born in East Yorkshire. Their birthplace was the bit between east and west which, to Artemis's everlasting confusion, was called North Yorkshire, just outside Selby. They were the only children of George and Grace, both on their second marriage. A middle-class family, owning their house, strong ties to the community and avid members of the Conservative Party. Their father, a police inspector, treated his family as if they were part of his division. As a young child, Caroline followed her father's example. She enjoyed ordering her little brother around, the annoying little boy who always asked her unanswerable questions. She continued to try and tell her obnoxious brother what to do and how to dress in their teenage years. That, much to the annoyance of their parents, ended up in constant arguing and bickering.

Caroline left home first to study at the London School of Economics. This left her brother with a few years of relative peace and quiet. Then Artemis followed her to London for his university education at Goldsmiths' College, because he had missed out on going to Durham University, which he had calculated as being as far away as possible from his sister.

Fate had ordained that they now settle in South-East London, while their widowed father remained in North Yorkshire.

"I want to make sure my little brother, who now lives alone, doesn't feel lonely and neglected. It's called caring for family."

"It's called interfering. What do you want today, as if I didn't know?"

Artemis had known for the last two months. His sister was trying to convince him to help her collate and analyse horse racing form, with the object of getting a winner at every race and making a fortune. She had the idea that his mind was analytical enough to make them successful gamblers.

As pleased as he was at her praise for his cerebral skills, he could not convince her that gamblers just do not win. Bookmakers win, gamblers lose, that was in Artemis's opinion a simple unbreakable fact of life. His sister however took the opposite view, having read a book that purported to show that blackjack tables in Las Vegas could be conquered. That is why she now described herself as a professional gambler, a title which Artemis knew to be wildly optimistic. Luckily for her, the husband she met at university, was a successful stockbroker and was able to circumnavigate her many losses.

"It can be done, Artemis. It's just a question of bringing together: the facts, the form, weather conditions, trainer's record, temperament of the horse and its personality to conclude which horse has the best chance of winning. There's a fortune to be made."

"Just look at the odds, the bookmakers have already done all the hard work. It's just any wealth that might be made will be theirs and theirs alone."

Artemis opened his book once again in the hope that his sister would take the hint and leave, but she carried on.

"I was reading on the internet that bookies decide which horse will be the favourite so that punters not in the know will go for it, when in fact they know an outsider will be first past the post. We just need to look at the same facts as them."

"You do realise there are very gullible people, not just in other countries, but in my kitchen as well."

"I'm just trying to help you after the divorce." Caroline picked up her pink phone from the table, stood up, pushed the chair backwards over the tiled floor, and then carefully replaced it. "But as ever, you think you know best. I'm off to work now."

Artemis looked up at his older sister, it was the first he had heard of a job. Tempted as he was to ignore the fact she had just revealed, the inquisitive side of his persona wanted to know more, even if it meant her staying with him a little longer.

"What job?"

Caroline smiled, pulled the chair back out and sat down again, excited to tell her brother about her part-time job. After university, she had for a while worked for a local accountant, preparing end-of-year accounts for small local businesses. She enjoyed the friendliness of the work, knowing her clients, understanding their challenges and weaknesses. She thought it far better than working at a large accounting firm uptown. They might pay more money, but such a job would be low on satisfaction.

Once married, she tried to have children, but none were forthcoming. As her husband earned more than enough to keep her and the house, he suggested that she might be better off not working in the hope that rest might make conceiving easier. It did no such thing, but instead led her to boredom and spending time online, gambling.

In the end it turned out that it was her husband who was the weak link in the baby-building chain. Together they decided that if God did not want them to have children, they were not going to use artificial means.

"Three afternoons a week with the company I worked with before. They were happy to take me back, help them out. They are still attracting new clients and with any luck it might end up full-time when there's enough business."

"What, doing the accounts for the self-employed?"

"Yes, that and helping tradesmen do their VAT returns. All easy stuff, but fun."

If Artemis needed any more evidence that his sister was not the full ticket, there it was. Whoever thought VAT returns could be described as fun. At least, now that she was back working, her interest in gambling might wane. The other advantage was that she might stay out of his hair more. Why he always used that well-worn saying, he could never really figure out, given that he shaved his head, although he stopped short of polishing it as well.

His baldness was by choice, not through illness. As a young man, he hated the amount of work his hair required. Washing it every morning, after which he could never trust it to go the way he wanted without using a hair dryer and he hated the heat. Then there were the constant adjustments needed during the day as gusts of wind, breeze, or even just walking, disturbed it. The final straw was the need to spend money every couple of weeks to have it cut back into his chosen style. A razor dragged over his head during every shower was a lot easier.

Before he could respond to his sister, the door chime echoed around the house. Not your normal dreary electronic tones for Artemis, his was an orchestral recording of 'Ode to Joy', thanks to a clever little app he had on his phone. This cutting-edge technology did little to impress Caroline.

"Why do you have such a poncy piece of music for a doorbell?"

"I am sure Ludwig Van Beethoven would not describe music from his ninth symphony as poncy, but I'm a tolerating individual. Be a dear and get that for me please?" Artemis smiled his best little boy lost one.

She got up in a huff and walked towards the front door. Sisters do have some uses, Artemis thought, as he returned to his book. He managed one paragraph before Caroline came back into the kitchen followed by Susan, whom he recognised. He assumed the man with her was her husband, Martin. With a sigh, he closed his book again.

"I gather this is business, so I'm off. See you later." Caroline acknowledged Susan and Martin as she left the room, closing the front door with a little too much enthusiasm, Artemis thought.

"Take a seat. I'd offer you one in the living room, but I haven't finished decorating. Hence, I'm sitting at the kitchen table enjoying a small glass of wine and a good book. I guess you have some news?"

After Martin and Artemis had been formally introduced to one another, Susan reported back on their day.

The conclusion that they had reached regarding Mrs Hall was that she was not in any form of collusion with her husband. She appeared to be a genuine grieving widow fearing what the future might hold, just as Artemis had predicted.

"What was strange was she mentioned that the insurance company had quizzed her already. Was that you?" Susan asked Artemis, who sounded a little coy when replying.

"Yes, I did speak to her. Quiz sounds a little harsh. Although I came to the same conclusion you have, I guess I wanted a second opinion. How about the undertakers?"

"Now there's a story good enough for the Sunday sleaze papers. The sacked employee was photographing dead bodies for some website, so he had to go. I guess in Barry Gladstone's view, another scandal was the last thing he wanted, hence the gossip on the street was that the guy lost his job over the body mix-up. Which didn't happen."

Artemis appeared to be underwhelmed by the employee problem, yet seemed to perk up and take notice when Susan said no bodies were mixed up or lost.

"What do you mean did not happen? Did they offer you any proof?"

Although Martin looked a little bored, Susan was full of excitement and racing ahead with the breakthrough. She told Artemis that in her view, the best friend, who discovered the body, was lying through his teeth.

"And if he is, then without doubt, Alan is alive somewhere. It's just finding that place and trying to understand the reason he wanted to appear dead."

"And where the body came from. We need to know that as well," Martin prompted.

"Ian Cook, you spoke to Ian Cook?" Artemis did not sound in the least pleased.

"Why not? He was the last person to see Alan alive and that's where all good detectives start."

"I never told you to speak to him, that was not part of the deal. All I asked was for you to speak to the widow and then the undertaker. Ian Cook was not part of the arrangement."

"Maybe not," Susan became defensive, "but you did employ the Hayden team to investigate. We leave no stone unturned."

Martin was fully aware that was the way Susan worked, not always using logic or being sensible, she just did what Susan did.

"Well, if you've spoken to him then I can't change that, but I'm very disappointed. Still, it could prove useful."

"You didn't ask us to speak to Ian Cook?" Martin asked, not knowing what had been agreed between them.

Susan answered before Artemis could, "My genius idea, if we're going to do a job, Martin, we should do it properly." It was obviously a reprimand. "And the key to this case is the identity of the only body we have. Now that's your department, Artemis. What do you have for us?"

It turned out he did not have much. The body was examined thoroughly by the local pathologist, who concluded it was a male, possibly in his late forties, a little overweight and not the healthiest example of a corpse that had been presented for an autopsy. Cause of death in layman's terms was a heart attack, not helped by the blackened lungs produced through years of smoking.

As for identification, so far that had drawn a blank. Fingerprints had provided nothing, zero from a couple of scars on the chest. The police also checked face recognition and dental records, all so far contributing zilch towards identifying the corpse, so he was continuing as John Doe for now.

Artemis explained that the police investigation had reached a hiatus. They'd sent the body back to the undertakers saying technically, as the death did not look suspicious, it was their property, which did nothing to help the situation. In effect the police had placed the whole thing on hold, not wishing to spend any more money or man-hours when they've far more pressing crimes to solve.

"It's their view that this is no more than an administrative error, which will balance out in the end. But, if you're saying Ian Cook is lying, then Alan is still alive.

"Identifying the dead body we have, would help us understand what really happened that night. We need to think outside of the box if we are going to unlock this mystery."

Artemis paused, waiting to see if the two detectives in front of him had any ideas that were better than the few he had.

"Check every interaction the body had with others," Susan offered, not sure if it was going to be the right answer. It was.

"Good idea. Maybe start with the ambulance staff, the ones who arrived in the middle of the night. They might have noticed something unusual." Artemis then added, "There's also something else I think you should know. Something I have only just found out, that might help, although I'm not sure it will."

It was incorrect to say he had only just found out. He knew before he met Susan the first time, it was just he didn't know how much importance to assign to it. But now that Susan and Martin felt the widow was an innocent party, they should be offered some doubt in that belief.

"It appears that five days after the, shall we say, the disappearance of Alan Hall, his wife's car was the innocent party in a very minor collision with another one in a Tesco car park. At the time, neither driver wanted to involve their respective insurance companies, the damage was minor.

"However, the guilty party, a woman who had driven into Mrs Hall's car, had a fit of righteousness and reported the accident to her insurance company anyway. No claim, she just wanted to be completely honest and frank with the insurers. She took the moral high ground. Odd, but there's no accounting for the whims of some people.

"The interesting part of her description of the accident, if you can even consider it such a thing, was that when she conversed with the driver, he was happy not to claim for damage."

"He?" Susan repeated.

"Yes, a male driver. It might be worth speaking to the lady who reported the accident, as well as the security team at Tesco, they might have some CCTV footage of who got out of Mrs Hall's car."

"Are you supposing that it was Alan driving?" Susan asked, while Martin was considering this whole thing was getting a little too complicated.

"Could be. As I've told you before, I can't go around asking questions, but I do have some details for you which might help." He pulled a sheet of paper from under his book. Fleetingly, he hesitated, which Susan thought odd.

"Back at the office, we can access a lot of information, which is out of reach to investigators like yourselves. Here." He handed the sheet to Susan who could see it was a printout of a mobile phone bill and a handwritten address.

"The highlighted number is the last call Alan made from his mobile phone, and that's the address of the person he called. It might be nothing, but we won't know until you've spoken to Mr Max Phillips, who was the last person to speak to Alan before his presumed death. Good luck."

Chapter 7

"Don't complain Martin, it was your idea to speak to the ambulance crew. The consequences are all yours."

"No, it wasn't," Martin argued back, "I simply mentioned it to you in the car. You suggested pursuing the body to Artemis, who advocated, too quickly in my opinion, the ambulance crew. In a way, I suspect he wanted us to speak to them. Are you sure he's not just using us to do his dirty work?"

Susan smiled, "Admit it, it's fun."

It had not been fun, but a somewhat difficult morning. Getting to the bottom of which medics attended the Hall residence on that fateful night, was akin to tricking the Government into giving out nuclear secrets. Two hours of waiting around before anyone with more than two pips on their shoulders would even consider speaking to them.

When they did finally speak to someone who had access to the information they wanted, they were treated like Russian spies asking for the keys to the Crown Jewels. The prospect of speaking to the ambulance crew looked unattainable. Until Susan mentioned they wanted to find the owner of the only body ever to escape from a coffin. Then the fortifications of bureaucracy crumbled.

The original event had resulted in more than a few tears of laughter in the canteen. The misfortune of the undertakers, ended in a spoof email sent to all staff, telling them to check their rearview mirrors every five minutes, to ensure passengers were still in place and not running behind the ambulance.

A quick call was made instructing the crew to wait, just continue their refreshment break until Susan and Martin arrived and they should cooperate with them.

Martin saw the Euro yellow ambulance as he pulled into the MacDonald's car park and carefully stopped beside it.

Instantly, Susan asked, "You hungry?"

"No!"

***

The two-man crew was standing beside their vehicle, making the most of the sunshine and the chance to stretch their legs. One of them was portly, and eagerly munching his way through a large hamburger. The other was taller, thin as a rake and had ears that looked as if he could sail away on them. Both had a warm welcoming smile for the detectives. It would make a change from treating patients.

The tall one, who introduced himself as Gerry, shook Susan's and Martin's hand with a degree of vigour that made the action almost an assault. He was the newbie on the team, only having been with the London Ambulance Service for just under six months. He had been fired from his previous job working in a pet shop.

The shorter partner, who had now finished his burger, gleefully pointed out that Gerry had been sacked for cleaning out the hamster cages, having first put the three hamsters in the snake tank. Gerry, at once protested that he thought the snake tank was empty at the time. An argument that his partner, Robert, and his previous employer dismissed.

Robert, on the other hand, had spent twenty years in the army before returning to civvy street. He had been driving an ambulance and patching up people for the last fifteen years, admitting, without being asked, that he favoured driving around a war zone than the streets of London. As he was clearly the senior partner in this working relationship, Robert, or Bob as he preferred, gave their version of events that night.

"It was in the early hours when we got the call. Person found unresponsive, so we popped along as quick as we could. The rapid response car was already tied up. But we didn't do bad, not much on the roads at that time of the morning. Turned up at the house, greeted by a bloke who showed us the casualty. We went through a small door at the side into a workshop.

"To be honest he was as dead as a doornail, I could see that as soon as I got down on the floor with him. But we still went through the motions, more for the benefit of the onlooker than the corpse. Gave what, about five minutes of pointless resuscitation? Then told the bloke, who had introduced himself as Ian, that his mate was dead.

"Gerry here, popped back to the van to let everyone know we had a stiff to deal with. It's not as though we can just leave the bloke, we needed a doctor and the police had to be informed. If people knew how much paperwork we have to do when they suddenly die at home, then I'm sure a lot would make more of an effort to get to a hospital before they expire.

"We were there, how long would you say, Gerry?"

"Couple of hours, I reckon."

"At least. If you want the exact time, we have a log and things. Copper turns up, young kid, sees the body and throws up. It was his first dead'un, poor sod. All night, he had a grey face, he'll learn. Asks a few questions and then declares it an accident. Well, it looked that way to me and Gerry, didn't it?"

Gerry nodded in agreement, not that after six months he had seen many dead bodies but was happy to accept what his more knowledgeable partner said.

"As I recall, we were left on site until the doctor and undertaker turned up. Quiet night, apart from that call, the days are the busy times. Anyway, they turn up, the doctor writes out the certificate, the undertaker sticks the body in the back of their van, and we're back on the streets. Simple, really."

Susan and Martin had expected that was what they were going to hear, so Bob's statement only confirmed their thoughts.

"From the moment you arrived," Martin asked, "until the undertakers took the body away, the deceased never left your sight?"

"Odd question. Ah, this is the bloke who fell out of the hearse, bloody hilarious that was. To answer your query, the corpse on the floor didn't move until the undertaker took him away. I bet there was another body in the back of the van, and they got 'em mixed up. Silly sods."

"And the other man, Ian, how was he all this time?" Susan asked, hoping that Martin would relent and let her eat here; she was getting hungry.

Once again, Robert was the main spokesperson for the duo.

"Always hard to tell, people deal with such tragic accidents in different ways. He was tense, wound up, quiet. Sat a lot of the time in the corner with a big frown."

"And the body, anything unusual about that?" Susan added, feeling as if she was grasping at straws.

"No, just a dead bloke on the floor. There was the wire that no doubt killed him, it had been unplugged. Apart from that, nothing."

Then Gerry joined the conversation, "What about the shirt?"

"It was a shirt, just a fancy one."

"What do you mean, shirt? Was there something different about it?" Martin aimed his question at Gerry, sensing that he was being left behind in this interview and wanted to be part of it.

"Only the make of it. It looked posh and the material was pretty good, it was a polo shirt with a Devred 1902 label. Never heard of them, but they're a French company. Looked them up and ordered myself one online."

"Is that it? A foreign shirt that you can buy over here?"

"Well, I'd never seen one before, so it was unusual."

"Yes," Robert added by way of reprimanding his junior, "in your eyes, it's unusual snakes eat hamsters, but shit happens, boy."

***

Harriet Holloway had lived in the same house all her life. A small, terraced one just off a complex junction called Fiveways. It was the junction that had completely fooled

Martin, who was now travelling down the main A20, currently a dual carriageway. Unfortunately, he was unable to turn around and have another go at dealing with Fiveways. In his view, it was not his fault, Susan disagreed.

"I told you second left, and I pointed with my finger in the direction you were meant to go."

"I was watching the road and not your finger, plus I did not appreciate there was a turning leading back almost the way we came."

"Even so, Martin, I did say second left. How that translates into going straight ahead, I've no idea."

"Because the road you were pointing at, I thought was the first left, then the second left must be going a crooked straight on. Plus, there was another turning to choose from."

"You did see my finger, I knew it. And the other turning, as you put it, was on your right, so it should have been discounted in your public-school logic when asked to turn left."

He was not going to admit it, but the complex junction was a little daunting. He hoped to navigate it better once he had found a place to turn around.

He managed to take the correct turning and a few moments later they parked outside Harriet's house.

Having spent her childhood and teenage years there, when her parents won a substantial sum of money on the National Lottery, they promptly transferred the house to their only daughter, bought a large sea-going yacht and now spent their days cruising the waters of the Mediterranean. Some thought it cruel, but Harriet was pleased as they had never shown much interest in her. Their actions gave her the opportunity to marry the man she loved, and her parents hated with a vengeance.

She came to the door holding her two-year-old daughter who looked flushed, having just finished a screaming fit. Harriet looked worried about two investigators wanting to talk to her about what had been a minor accident.

She guided the investigators into her cosy living room and placed her daughter into a playpen that seemed to dominate it. Part of her wished she had not admitted the accident to her insurance company, but she knew it was the right thing to do, whatever the result.

"It was a horrible day," Harriet recounted. "Rain and wind, one of those dreary days when you just want to stay inside. But I had to go shopping, little miss had run out of nappies. Plus, I had forgotten the Soy sauce for a dish I was doing that night. Hence, I put little miss in the car and off I go to Tesco. The rain was persistent all the way there and while I was trying to park as well.

"I was reversing into a space, when another car comes up real close and is waiting impatiently. Then little miss has one of her screaming fits, it's the 'terrible twos', you know.

"I got flustered, and as I turned, missed how close I was to a car which was already parked. I scraped the front wing. I could have screamed, but no one would have heard me over the noise she was making in the back of the car.

"Finally, I parked, then jumped out and went over to the car I had hit, expecting the worst, some angry driver effing and jeffing. Thankfully, the passenger window was open and I leaned in. The man couldn't have been nicer, 'Don't worry miss, it's only a bit of paint, a bit of T-cut and it should be fine. Call it a knock for a knock.'

"Relieved, I couldn't tell you how relieved I was. Mind, I did as a precaution take a note of his number, just in case. I thought it only wise."

"Then you had an attack of the guilts?" Susan asked.

"You could say that. What if he'd mentioned it to his insurance company, it could look bad on my record, so I reported it. Was that the wrong thing to do?"

Martin was not going to offer any advice; he would have been inclined to ignore the whole thing. As he listened, it was clear she referred each time to the driver as a 'he'. To make certain, he asked, "If you are positive it was a man, what did he look like?"

"I'm categorically sure it was a man; I wasn't that shaken up. But he was just a man, maybe thirty, maybe a bit more or a bit less, I'm terrible with that sort of thing. Just a very average man."

"Did he wear glasses?" Susan asked, having watched more TV detectives than Martin, she could reel off a list of standard questions that investigators used.

"No, I don't think so."

"Beard or clean shaven?" Susan tried the question, the previous being a waste of time.

"It was kind of a dark day, and it wasn't bright in the car. Can't be sure. But he did have a tattoo on his finger, which I thought odd."

"What sort of design was it?" Susan asked, sensing a breakthrough.

"I would describe it as a diamond shape. Like you get on a pack of cards."

"Like two triangles stuck together," Martin waded in.

"Yes, exactly."

"Well, thank you, Mrs Holloway, you have helped us. We shouldn't need to trouble you again." Martin wanted to conclude the interview, which to his disappointment seemed to have provided Susan with a new clue. His wish was strengthened when little miss in the playpen started to grizzle, her volume on the rise.

***

Even though he had tried to deter Susan, her hunger and the associated complaining had forced Martin to give in. But not before they had spoken to the security team at the Tesco supermarket and viewed the relevant CCTV footage. At least that was completed, unfortunately this Tesco superstore had a café. He nursed a black coffee as Susan bit into a toasted ham ciabatta, with an eagerness that frankly evaded him.

The security team was helpful, directing them towards a small room on the first floor of the building. Once there among the small TV screens, they made it clear what they wanted. The first response was, 'You're very lucky, another day or two and we'd have wiped the tapes.'

Martin nodded, he knew without doubt they were not actual flimsy tapes, it was just the way everyone seemed to describe the capture of CCTV images on a hard drive. Maybe using the word tape was a nostalgia quirk, 'reformatting the hard drive' sounded a lot less romantic in a security guard sort of way.

The monitoring room at this extra-large Tesco supermarket was compact to say the least. It was not helped by the fact the security guard in charge of the CCTV was a large man. Plus, the room was designed for one person sitting alone for hours on end, not for guests.

The operator was called Howard. An obese man in his late fifties wearing a stained, untidy uniform. His weight resulted from the hours he spent sitting in front of the ten television screens watching for shoplifters, pickpockets and any other sort of criminality that might be in vogue.

Howard was known to be very protective of his recordings. Normally only police officers could view the data without a formal written request. Anyone, including Tesco staff, needed prior authorisation in line with the Data Protection Act, which Howard quoted many times. For Martin and Susan though, Howard made an exception as he had never worked with a private investigator before and found the whole thing rather exciting. Hence no paperwork was required.

In the end Howard's cooperation proved to be useful, a lot more than the CCTV footage they viewed. It turned out that Tesco was more protective of its stock than what goes on in the car park. A single camera covering the entrance, recorded the comings and goings of shoppers throughout the day. Jumpy, grainy images of cars, vans and bikes entering and then no doubt leaving.

Having the correct day and the approximate time enabled Howard, after a few minutes, which seemed like hours to Martin, in the cramped environment, to find the Ford Focus of Mrs Hall entering the car park. Freezing and magnifying the image did little to offer any form of valid identification, but there looked like a man driving and a woman sitting in the passenger seat. After another interminable fifteen minutes, they located the car in question leaving the car park, this provided even less information. Even though Martin thanked Howard, he knew it had been a waste of time.

"I've an idea," Susan suddenly let out, as she swallowed a large chunk of toasted ciabatta. "Let's go back and ask Howard to see what customers came in soon after the car arrived. That way we'd see if it was Alan or his wife, or even both coming into the shop."

"Don't you think that's like looking for a needle in a haystack? We know already it must have been the lady in the car who went shopping, the man was on his own when Harriet scraped the Ford Focus.

"It's becoming clear Mr and Mrs Hall are in some sort of scam in which he disappears. She must have been lying to us. Obviously, the insurance is not paying out now, but only because the body fell out of the coffin, otherwise they probably would have."

Martin felt he had proposed a suitable scenario which answered several questions and would soon, hopefully later that day, mean they could stop this asinine task of running around making pointless enquiries. He did have a holiday in Italy planned and there was shopping for new clothes to be attended to. At the back of his mind, he wondered if Susan had another hypothesis. Of course, she did.

"The trouble with you Martin, is that you haven't watched enough television detectives to know about scams and trickery." Susan wiped a blob of mayonnaise from her plate with the last small piece of ciabatta, popped it into her mouth and began to offer her hypothesis as she ate. "There have been many cases of people faking their own deaths to cash in on an insurance policy, not an uncommon crime. But..."

"There's always a but," Martin said, with a tired voice.

"But none of those cases involved an actual body. Normally people go missing at sea or in the wilderness. In this case, we have a body. Who commits a murder to fake their own death? Plus, the best friend identifying the body makes no sense whatsoever, unless we accept that he's lying as I thought, and is in on the plan. And before you ask, I have no idea what the plan might be, but at the bottom of this case, I think there's a murder."

"Maybe we should call the police," Martin answered, pushing his now empty cup towards the centre of the table. "But there's no need, they already have the body which died of a heart attack and even they have shoved it to one side. I guess they think it's, as everyone else seems to, a case of jumbled-up dead bodies. Unless my wife knows different?" Which at once he regretted saying, she always had another idea.

"Here," Susan unfolded the sheet of paper that Artemis had given her, the mobile telephone record for Alan Hall's alleged last day on Earth. She pushed it toward Martin and stabbed the paper with her finger.

"That phone call holds the key to this case."

"Like the dead body; or was that the wrong key?"

"Okay, I promise that unless our visit to this bloke uncovers vital evidence, I will tell Artemis we're done, and I will join you in shopping for holiday clothes."

Martin thought that was a fair compromise for Susan. They left Tesco and headed for the home of Max Phillips.

Chapter 8

The house was a substantial property. Detached, with a large front garden full of different types of evergreen shrubs, some of which had hues that were not green, more a mix of red and orange tints. Whatever their colour, they were all well-kept. It was modern, almost new, certainly built in the current decade, with brickwork that was uniform and lacked personality. It might have been a big house, but the exterior was bland.

The red-painted wooden door was answered by a tall Asian man, thin limbs and with a cautious attitude to visitors he had never seen before. He was not Mr Phillips. As they did not have an appointment, he would first ask Mr Phillips if he had time to speak to them. They confirmed that they just wanted a quick word about a phone call that was made to him by an Alan Hall, who had recently died. Susan wanted to add that he might not be dead but thought that might only complicate matters. They were left on the doorstep with the door firmly closed.

A moment or two later, the Asian man admitted the couple into the hallway, making it clear their visit should be short as Mr Phillips was a busy man. They followed the long legs of the doorman into a large study at the back of the house. Susan noticed his right hand appeared to be missing a thumb. It made his hand look slimline.

They were shown into a square, bright room, with plain magnolia-painted walls and a beige carpet that was spotless given its pale colour. A large open patio door led out onto a paved terrace. A faux fireplace, with what looked to be real logs in the hearth. Seated at a modern chrome-framed desk with a clear-glass top was Max Phillips, who smiled warmly at his visitors as he pointed to a long beige sofa opposite him.

"Please take a seat; you have intrigued me. A phone call from an Alan Hall? Please tell me more," he said, as he folded his copy of the Racing Post he had been reading when his guests walked in.

Max Phillips was a plump man in his sixties, a rounded face with jowls that hung down and merged with his thick neck. The most striking thing about him was his attire. He was sitting at his desk in a white fedora with a red and orange colour band. This band almost matched the blazer he was wearing which had red and yellow vertical stripes, bright, if not brighter than the room itself. His bow tie was also in a coordinating colour. Red corduroy trousers concluded the distinctive style of Mr Phillips.

"We are investigating the death of a Mr Hall, who died of natural causes recently," Martin tried to make the whole thing sound as casual as possible. "According to his phone record, your mobile was the last number he called. Do you know Mr Hall?"

Max frowned a little as he appeared to think, then shook his head.

"I don't think I know anyone called Hall, but it's a common name and at my age I have met a lot of people. When was he supposed to have called me?"

Susan referred to her sheet of paper, then shared the date and time with Max, who once again paused to think back.

"Ah, the time gives it away; just before midnight. Was it that long ago? My, how time flies. I was in bed, reading before I put out the light and my mobile phone rang. I didn't recognise the number but answered anyway.

"As I recall he was asking if he could speak to someone called Jeff. Respectfully, I pointed out it wasn't my name, and I didn't know of a Jeff connected with my number. He apologised and that was the end of the call. It can be difficult with modern phones, it's so easy to punch in the wrong number, especially if you have podgy fingers like me."

"And that was it?" Susan asked.

"Yes. If you have his phone record there, I imagine it shows a very short call. But you say the poor man is now dead, I do hope Jeff was not his doctor or something and I contributed to his demise in some way."

"Nothing like that," Susan replied, wanting to reassure this old man who was clearly concerned. "Well, I say he died, we're trying to establish if he really is dead. You must have heard about the story of the wrong body falling out of the coffin."

"My god, yes, I did read about that. Was that the same man who called me?"

"Alan Hall called you, but it wasn't his body in the coffin," Susan tried to make things clearer.

"Now I recall there was a mix-up with bodies, was one of them the Alan Hall who called me? How very sad for the family. But to be honest, I'm a little chuffed, being part of a story in the news. We all lead such mundane lives, don't we? Well, not you investigators. I'm just sorry I can't help you more. Would I be right in thinking the two of you are looking for the other dead body which must, by logical deduction, mean you are searching for Alan Hall?"

"In a manner of speaking we are," Susan admitted. "Although it seems that he might well still be alive."

"Alive? I thought you said he was dead."

"Don't worry. We're just assuming that without a body he could still be alive," Martin answered. "You've cleared up another little matter in our quest. We won't keep you any longer. Thank you for your time."

"My pleasure. I do hope you are successful in finding Mr Hall, dead or alive. It sounds like a complex case; I wish you good luck. My man, Archibald, will show you out."

***

Martin was pleased that was the end. Nothing had been gained from the last phone call and now it was time to consider a shopping list of clothes. He would call Norton and Sons in the morning and arrange an appointment. Maybe a late afternoon visit followed by dinner in town. He wanted to look his best for what he considered to be honeymoon part two.

"I'll let you call Artemis and tell him the news. Thank him, tell him it was mildly entertaining, but we can't help him further with Mr Hall."

"What are you talking about? We have the lady who was in the funeral car with Christine Hall to speak to next." Susan started to tap the address into the satellite navigation system.

"That was not the agreement I made with you in Tesco. You said if the visit to Max Phillips uncovered nothing new, then we were finished."

"Well, it did reveal some new evidence."

"What are you talking about? It was a wrong number."

"Yes. But if it was really a wrong number, Alan Hall would have made another call to the person he wanted to speak to. Mr Phillips is lying."

***

Sharon Taylor was not surprised to have two private investigators walk into her house. In a way she had been expecting them, although she had not mentioned her fear to Christine. The poor woman had enough going on in her life as it was.

She was only three months older than Christine and they had been friends since secondary school. No one expected them to become pals, not with Christine coming from her semi-detached middle-class background with a father who could afford to buy a new car every three years, 'avoid the boring MOT' as he put it. Although none of Christine's classmates could understand what her father did for a living, something in the city in the banking sector? Even Christine had no real concept of what he did.

Sharon's father was a refuse collector, started work at six in the morning and finished by two in the afternoon. Spent the next three hours in the pub and expected his dinner on the table as he walked in at five-fifteen, you could almost set your watch by his arrival at the Formica dinner table.

Their spacious council house was cluttered with 'valuable' scrap that her father recovered from the bins he emptied, citing that people sometimes have no idea the value of their rubbish. Sharon accepted that all parents are strange in their own way, hence Christine and Sharon made the most of their friendship.

"It was a shock," Sharon admitted, as Susan and Martin asked about the accident and subsequent fall out, as Susan put it, using a poor choice of words.

"I suppose any car crashing is shocking enough, but to see the coffin tumble out of the hearse and break open, well, it's the stuff of nightmares. Then to see a body flail across the road like some rag doll, that image will live with me forever.

"Christine had turned away; she always said she never wanted to see Alan dead, she has said it time and time again. Her last image of him, she wanted to be one where he was chatting and laughing. But when I saw the face, well, what could I do? I had to tell her."

Martin watched as Sharon sat on the edge of her Parker Knoll chair, fidgeting with a silk scarf that she kept sliding between her fingers. She looked anxious, almost scared. He wondered what was behind her nervous disposition.

"What did Christine say when she understood that it was not her husband on the road?" He asked.

"If anything, she sounded relieved that it wasn't her husband. But then she got angry, upset. It was all to do with where he was. She began shouting, almost hysterically, 'Who's that lying there?' It took a bit to calm her down, who could blame her?"

"What do you think happened?" Martin was wondering if Sharon had a theory of her own.

"I don't know, I guess they just lost Alan. Didn't they?"

"Do you have a theory?" Now it was Susan who could see a line of questions that might get to what was troubling Sharon. Susan had also noticed the nervous disposition of the school friend. A friend who had known Christine for many years. They had been on holiday together, shopped till they dropped together, attended parties, and gossiped at wine bars; they were true friends. But here was a friend who looked as if she knew a secret and was trying to cover it up for the sake of her buddy.

"Why would I have a theory?"

"Come on, Sharon," Susan persisted, "if we hear of an unnamed MP who has been accused of something, we all have a theory as to who it might be. What do you think has happened to Alan?"

"How would I know? I only know what people have said about it."

"Do you think Alan is alive somewhere?" The question was blunt, but Susan waited for an answer as Sharon twisted her scarf frantically between her fingers.

"Why would he be alive? They said he was dead. So, he must be dead, mustn't he?"

"Unless he just wanted to appear dead." This time, Martin could see clearly that Sharon felt trapped in a corner.

"Do you think he's alive?" Sharon pushed the question straight back at the investigators.

Susan looked at Martin; he did not think he had, but later Susan said he gave her a signal.

"Yes, we think he's alive, but he needs a reason to want to disappear. You wouldn't happen to know that reason, would you?"

"First of all, I don't know. It's just..." she hesitated, not confident. The moment they had walked in, she knew she would need to share her hypothesis. It was something she was looking forward to off-loading to someone, but maybe not investigators. Still, they were here in front of her asking the question. "...I've never trusted Alan." There, she had said it openly, there was no turning back. "He always looks at you as if he's undressing you, thinking about what is under your clothes. He made me feel very uncomfortable and I always tried to avoid being alone with him. He never tried anything on, but, for instance, if my husband and I were out with him and Christine, Alan could make some lurid remark, which everyone laughed at, but I always felt it wasn't just joking around."

"So, to your mind, he might have faked his death to run off with another woman."

"Please don't mention this to Christine. I would hate her to know what I'm thinking, it would break her heart. But he was, I thought, untrustworthy."

"Do you know if he ever had an affair?"

"Christine never mentioned such a thing, or any suspicions she had. But he and his so-called best friend, Ian, regularly spent a couple of nights at a pub. Christine just thought it was a boys' night out. But on the occasions my husband and I joined her and Alan at that pub, The Cross Swords, for a social night out, he seemed very friendly with the bar staff, especially the female ones. Overly friendly."

Even Martin could see, despite his indifferent approach to Alan being dead or alive, that what Sharon was telling them cast a whole new light on the case. Another woman could be a motive. Discard the old wife then run off into the sunset with the girlfriend. That would make sense, but for the doubts that still resided in his mind. Also, he was starting to have worries about ever getting to Verona.

Martin knew people were not living under Victorian values, divorce was common enough nowadays, plus Alan would have got half the house to start his new life. But what would force him into a new life with a new identity?

Then there was the ever-present question of the body, the yet unidentified one. As Susan had rightly pointed out, if you are going to fake your own death, why go to all the trouble of finding a body? Martin was having trouble linking the dots, that being the case, there had to be more dots to make up the whole picture.

Susan, on the other hand, had already added a few more dots to her picture. They might have just learnt about Christine in a car with a man they assumed to be Alan. But now it occurred to her that it might not have been him, maybe Christine's lover?

"What about Christine, if she was having an affair, would she tell her best friend?" She asked.

Sharon would make a bad poker player. Her eyes dilated in fear, her body went rigid, and her fingers turned white as she tightened the innocent scarf around her hand.

"You'd best ask her."

Susan planned to. She was also sure of what the truth might be.

Then there was another question that Susan wanted some clarity on.

"Who was the school friend that Christine was with the night that Alan died? Clearly it wasn't you as we aren't in Crawley."

"Maureen Keady, we all went to the same school. I know Christine had gone over to stay for a couple of nights, helping with the garden."

"And the friend that Christine stayed with following her husband's alleged death?"

That question was not easy for Sharon. She knew the answer but equally knew it was not her place to say. "You'd best ask Chris."

As Susan led Martin back to his car, she was racking up a list of questions she wanted to ask the supposed widow of Alan Hall.

Chapter 9

"It won't take long. Only about ten minutes, that's all. I've checked it's in stock."

Martin knew from bitter experience that no shopping trip where Susan was concerned lasted ten minutes.

They had left Sharon and her strangled scarf with what they considered a solid plan that would progress their investigation. A visit to Alan's place of work might reveal a colleague who would be happy to share any gossip, or indeed offer knowledge of any extra-marital affairs that he or his wife might be having. It was becoming increasingly likely that the Halls were each engaged with their own extra-marital affair.

The downside to this plan, Martin soon found out, was that they were to pass within half a mile of an IKEA superstore, where Susan, having been reassured by Christine, now wanted to buy a chair for the spare room.

Since moving in, Susan had taken to the process of furnishing their new home with an eagerness that pleased Martin. Although he was more than happy not to be involved in any such domestic chores, he was dragged into them by her at every opportunity.

Hence, he was now parking in a car park that he suspected was the size of Wembley Stadium. Judging by the number of vehicles that populated the area he feared that the interior of IKEA was going to be akin to a football match. Not that he had ever been to a football match at Wembley, he had only seen the news reports and they had been enough to put him off attending.

He followed Susan into the store, up the long staircase, where he was confronted by multiple room settings, piles of tea lights, plus people in numbers that troubled him.

"Okay, what are we looking for?" he asked as he bumped into a woman with a large yellow bag over her shoulder. Yellow bags seemed to be very popular with IKEA shoppers and he felt a little underdressed without one.

"The same chair that Christine had, the one she was sitting in. Looked good I thought. It'll fit nicely into the corner by the window."

"I hope this won't take long; we've still got to pay a visit to Potts Field airport."

"They work nights, so we have plenty of time," she reminded Martin, as he trailed behind her.

Martin followed Susan past displays of living room and dining areas. Then she appeared to take him through someone's bedsit, which proclaimed just how much storage fitted into the living area. Not that it impressed Martin in the least. The only wardrobe he could see was nowhere near enough for a gentleman to hang all his clothes.

Finally, they stopped in an area of the shop that resembled an airport lounge, a first class one, due to the high ratio of large leather sofas spread around. Martin recognised the chair that Susan had her heart set on. Not because he recalled it from Christine's house, rather it was the way Susan sprawled over it with a smug smile.

"What do you think?" She waved Martin to join her on the matching armchair. Susan's was brown leather. Martin sat politely on the black leather version.

"Landskrona, is that where it was made?" Martin asked as he read the large label dangling from the arm of what he considered to be a very comfortable seat.

"I doubt it. It's what they call it, the model's name. Like your Honda Civic, this is an IKEA Landskrona. We also need a Billy bookcase."

"Is that from here?" Martin asked fearing Susan had another store in mind on the way to the airfield.

"Yes, it's a corner bookcase that will fit behind the door."

"Not a very Swedish name is it," Martin said, stating the obvious.

"Maybe they ran out of Swedish words. I don't suppose they have many in their language."

Martin was not sure if that was a fact. What he did know was that Swedish shoppers must enjoy walking, or to be more precise, a day's trek. After they had arranged delivery of the armchair, they were given directions as to where the Billy bookcase was hiding. They walked, then walked some more, before going down steps into what appeared to be a totally different shop called Market Place.

Susan reassured him it was still part of IKEA. Then after what Martin considered to be a slog through an obstacle course of household utensils and soft furnishings, they arrived at a junction which convinced Martin they were lost, they must have taken a wrong turning between the duvets and rugs. They had ended up in the IKEA stockroom, having missed the 'Staff Only' signs. In fact, it was the stockroom to which the public were admitted to self-serve. Martin compared it to a supermarket for giants. Susan ignored his childish comments and went in search of Aisle 24 and her Billy bookcase.

If Martin thought the ordeal of IKEA shopping once they pushed the trolley through the self-serve tills was over, he was wrong. Having seen the length of the three packages Susan had bought, he wondered if they would ever fit in his car. They did, but closing the hatchback was impossible and required the use of stolen string from the self-service wrapping counter.

Whilst he was carefully securing Susan's newest purchase in the back of his car, hoping he had tied the knots strongly enough to hold everything in place, Susan popped back into the store with the excuse she had forgotten something. Her procurement of a bag of frozen meatballs only cast further doubt onto Martin's assumption that IKEA was a furniture store.

***

It was now dark. Potts Airfield was, as the name implied, a big field where light aircraft landed on a rough grass runway. During the day it was populated by enthusiasts, private pilots and geeks who noted aircraft registration numbers. The small café, with walls adorned by pictures of aircraft past and present, was a meeting place, almost a quasi-club room, where, in the main, men discussed the finer points of flying and recalled difficult challenging flights.

At night the large chicken wire gates were half-closed, mainly because the open half was hanging precariously on a broken hinge. There were no lights, but for a small glow emitting from the portacabin that abutted the currently closed café.

To the left of the gates was a large, weathered sign affixed to the fence welcoming you to Potts Airfield. Apart from the inanimate sign, there was an old man, seated on a small foldable stool. He was wrapped in a thick heavy coat, with a black scarf wrapped tightly around his neck and a large woolly hat that he had pulled over his ears. Leaning against his legs were three handwritten dog-eared cardboard signs.

The first simply said: 'No Expansion', the second, looking a little newer in the half light, proclaimed: 'Aliens are landing', the final placard read: 'Prepare to defend'.

After passing a general comment on the protester, pointing out he was not going to get a lot of footfall at this time of night, Martin carefully parked his car close to the portacabin, between a smart looking white Mazda MX5 sports car and a Ford Focus ST. Both recent models and built for speed, not economy. After checking his tied-down cargo, relieved that the knots were holding fast, he walked with Susan towards the door of the portacabin, then knocked politely and waited.

The door opened, causing a rush of moist warm air to wash over them. The man standing in front of them was about six feet tall, had an egg-shaped face with receding black hair. His eyebrows looked unnaturally bushy. He wore jeans and a high visibility jacket over a checked shirt. He looked at the two of them. Visitors at this time of night were rare, if not unheard of.

"Sorry, the airfield is closed," he informed them, without any emotion attached to his voice.

"We guessed that. We're here to see the night crew," Susan proffered with a smile.

"And the reason you want to see the night crew?" He now sounded a little more wary of these nocturnal visitors.

They explained they were there to talk about Alan, who had once been part of the night crew. They also clarified who they were and that they were interested in the events of the night Alan died. Declaring themselves as investigators had done nothing to allay the distrustful look in his eyes. Even so, he invited them into the cramped portacabin and offered them a seat.

There was another man already in the cabin leaning back on a swivel chair, his feet resting on a worktop as he read a newspaper. He acknowledged the presence of the newcomers and went back to his paper, apparently indifferent as to who, why or what was going on.

The room was rectangular in shape, with a worktop stretching from the door, under the window, to the end of the building, where the reclining man turned a page of his tabloid and continued perusing. On it was a mess of tools, oddments of machinery, tins of paint, hand cleanser and a farrago of other odds and ends.

The back wall had four scruffy lockers, a small dirty table with a selection of cups on it, plus a kettle and various beverage bags. Martin had no plans to accept the offer of a drink from that table. Susan also refused, although the half-empty packet of McVitie's Hobnobs did tempt her, yet somehow she resisted, having noticed the grimy hands of the man in front of her.

Bill Latham, who had opened the door to them, introduced himself. He was happy to confirm that he was the person who regularly worked alongside Alan Hall. He told them he had fallen off his motorbike, damaged his knee and had only returned to work last week, consequently, he was not on duty the night Alan died.

He stood in front of Martin and Susan, who both declined the offer of sitting, for fear of getting grease, oil, or whatever had stained the chairs on their clothes. Plus, as far as Martin could see, they were not going to stay long.

Bill was one of those people who liked to talk without, it would seem, breathing between sentences. Following on from the news item of his bike accident, he told them he had spent four hours in A&E only to be told, 'go home and rest'.

His bike suffered little damage. It was a variety of Triumph, which was about as much as Martin was interested in. It turned out it was the same bike Bill was riding – it was one of three Triumphs that he had restored over the years – when he first met Alan. It was beginning to sound like a love story.

Apparently, Alan's own Triumph bike had been purchased from a dealer and therefore didn't restore himself. The implication, Martin thought, made Alan less of a lover of motorbikes than Bill. Susan assumed from listening to Bill waxing lyrical about meeting Alan, it must have been rose-coloured. It was Bill who told Alan about a job on the night crew at the airfield.

Going off on a tangent, Bill explained in a little too much detail for Martin, what the night crew got up to. It sounded a lot, but Martin guessed from the state of the broken front gates and the tatty portacabin they were in, the night crew were never overworked. He recalled that it was Alan and Ian who popped home during the night shift, nothing could have been pressing at the airfield that night.

Susan, on the other hand, had begun to feel sorry for the man reading his newspaper, no doubt ignoring all that was being said because he had heard it many times before.

It took a little persuasion before Bill got down to answering the question that Susan had asked earlier in the proceedings, "What sort of guy was Alan?"

"Salt of the earth was Alan. Always happy to help you and go that bit further if need be. Take my accident, he was the one who popped along and picked up my bike for me, put it in the back of a van. No idea where he got the van from, but that was Alan for you, he'd find a way to get things done. Nothing was too much trouble. He didn't just collect the bike, which was only scraped along the petrol tank and the handles got a little bit bent, but even picked up the broken glass and stuff that had been swept into the gutter. He knew how us renovators like to have all the original materials on the bike. Can't be having modern bits, it's just not the same."

"What about his social life, were there any other ladies on the side?"

"Christ no. Alan playing around, he wasn't the type, straight as a die that way. He'd go out and have a drink with the blokes. We used to meet up last Sunday of the month out on our bikes, Surrey Triumph Riders, that's the name of the club. We'd meet at the same place. I've been going there for years, Alan hasn't, but I am now one of the long stayers at the club, was even treasurer at one time, did a three-year stint on that one. We'd have a few beers after the ride. Yes, Alan would have a few out with the lads, but no shenanigans with the ladies. He was just not the type. Loved his wife, well why not, bit of a looker is Christine, although I shouldn't say it, but she is."

"What about her?" Susan asked. "Do you think she might be playing away from home?"

For the first time since they had entered the room, Bill paused to think about what he was going to say, which surprised them, it had to mean something.

"Well, I don't usually like to speculate or share gossip. But Alan did say to me once that he thought she might be seeing her boss, the plumber person that she works for. But that doesn't really matter now does it? Him being dead and all."

"But what if he decided to fake his own death?"

"Alan? Don't be daft, he had too much to lose. Nice house, good-looking wife, well-paid job here, which is not the hardest in the world if I'm honest. He was set up for life. Fake his death, no way. If he was going to do that, he would have told me, I'm sure of it.

"Plus, his best mate, Ian, the one who helped him out while I was off with my knee, he phoned the ambulance; and saw him dead on the floor. No way could he be mistaken. If he was lying, then who would the body on the floor be if it wasn't Alan. No, hundred per cent he's dead, just bloody mislaid somehow."

Bill seemed, just like everyone else they had spoken to, sure that Alan would not have any reason or motive to fake his own death. He seemed, on the face of it, to be living a comfortable life, but for the hint that his wife might be having an affair. That was possibly a fly in the ointment. Then there was his last phone call, a wrong number.

"If we told you that we think Alan is alive someplace, it would surprise you?" Susan asked, as she believed that to be true and the more people who knew her theory the better, one of them might make a slip or even confess if she was lucky.

"If that's the case, then his mate must be in on it all. Plus, who was dead on the floor? That's one odd scenario you are suggesting to me. I don't want to be telling you how to do your job, but I can't see how you came up with that."

"And you can't think of any reason why Alan might want to disappear?" Susan knew that she had already asked it, but she had seen on the Rockford Files, asking the same question twice to the same person can present a clue.

He shook his head. "As I said, can't think of any reason, he had it all. Why would he go off and start a new life? It just doesn't make sense."

They thanked Bill for his time, hoping in a sarcastic way that they had not wasted too much of it.

Then standing at the door Susan asked, "That bloke at the gate, what's that all about? A one-man protest?"

"He's harmless enough. We had a few more protesters a while back. The airfield bosses were thinking of having a real runway laid. Get more business jets, you know those private Lear jets and stuff. There's money to be made in that sort of work. And we're well placed here, close to the capital and all that. The local residents didn't see it that way. When the Potts Field management put in for planning permission, there were constant protests about the expansion, which went on for a couple of months. In the end, the council said no, they weren't going to allow this little airfield to become a business hub for the rich.

"All the residents then went off and celebrated, but the old man stayed on, making sure we didn't concrete the field when no one was looking. And also, he has this thing about alien landings, little green men preparing to take over the earth or some such nonsense. But as I say, he's harmless enough. He lives alone, his wife died years ago, think he's a little lonely really. He does about three hours a day, mainly in the early evening. We take him a cup of tea and a sandwich once in a while, you know the out-of-date sandwiches from the café. I think he's in his seventies now, so we keep an eye on him, it can get cold during the evening. Then again, maybe he's just taking us for a ride, free food and drink and all that." Bill laughed.

As Martin drove out, after checking the knots on his IKEA parcels once more, he waved at the old man, who smiled, returning his wave.

"It takes all sorts to make up the world," Susan said, in a philosophical sort of way which was totally out of character for her.

Martin ignored the comment as he saw the first few spots of rain start to fall on the windscreen. He needed to get home. He was sure that soggy cardboard around Susan's Billy units was not going to be well received by her.

Chapter 10

Sitting at the kitchen table, Martin crunched his buttered toast noisily as he read the Telegraph. There were, he would admit, a lot of disadvantages to living in the virtually isolated village of Highfield, but the one big advantage was the paperboy. The local newsagent still employed a youth to cycle around the detached houses pushing daily newspapers through letterboxes. An English tradition that Martin felt should be made compulsory. There was something reassuring about holding a broadsheet in your hand while eating breakfast.

Although even paperboys or girls for that matter, complete their rounds now on electric bikes, nothing like the old days, when cycling around in all weathers had been a healthy occupation. Not that Martin had ever taken part in such errands, but he had known others who did.

Susan sat opposite, phone in hand, scrolling through messages, Facebook posts and the inevitable horoscope which he knew was always a feature of the morning repast. She finished her apricot Danish pastry, then smiled at her husband.

"Best put the paper down, it's time to find out what's going to happen to you today."

Martin sighed, placed his paper on the table and waited. Before Susan could begin the doorbell rang. They looked at each other with unspoken questions. Who is that? Who will answer it? Susan, being the naturally inquisitive type, was first up from the table and moving towards the front door as Martin picked up his paper and continued an article on the new Honda Civic. If Susan was getting a new kitchen, then it was only fair that he had a new car.

"Our builder is here," Susan pronounced, as she followed a young, bearded man into the kitchen. Sam Baxter, owner and only director of Baxter Builders Company, beamed at Martin.

"Soon have this room looking totally different, only take a couple of weeks. It'll be a dream for the missus to do the cooking in."

He was offered tea, milk, three sugars – then he joined Martin and Susan at the table.

"Just wanted to let you know we have all the units now at our warehouse. And here's the good news, we can start the day after tomorrow."

"Was that in the plan?" Martin queried, having put his research for a new car to one side.

"No, but I've had a cancellation and can start the day after tomorrow. Good news, eh?"

Martin looked at Susan for guidance. To his mind the kitchen being ripped out in the next day or so did not fit in with his plans, with or without an investigation. Susan looked as nonplussed as he did.

"The thing is," Martin started, "we have made all our plans based on you not starting in a day or so, but starting as planned."

Sam picked up a biscuit from the table, dunked it in his tea, placed the whole Hobnob in his mouth, then halfway through chewing started speaking, "Get yer drift totally but, there's always a but, sorry. If I put off doing your job now, the next one lasts six weeks, so I'll need to delay your start date by about a month. Just the way things work out sometimes, balancing the demands of clients. So, if I can start yours the day after tomorrow, you'll get your finished dream kitchen early, and it's looking good, your wife has some great ideas. Her ideal kitchen will be ready in three weeks."

"But we're going away, that was how we planned it."

"Understand, can't be without the kitchen, who can? Bathrooms are the same, can't do without a loo for a couple of weeks. That's why we'll factor in your needs to our work schedule. Each night you'll have a kitchen you can use, might not be pretty but you won't starve. That's the thing, can't have my clients starving."

Once again, Martin looked towards Susan, who had taken up the role of project manager, hence he hoped she would speak up soon, she did.

"No problem, Sam, the sooner the better. Would you like some toast?"

"Oh lovely, any chance of a few beans to go with it, so dry without, I think."

There was a very small part of Martin that suggested it might be better to move back in with Mother for the next couple of weeks, avoiding the inevitable chaos. Also, there would be a far greater number of good restaurants to choose from.

"Where're you going?" Sam asked as he cut into his beans on toast.

"Verona," Susan answered. She did, to Martin's delight, sound excited.

"Nice place. Went there once for a long stag weekend. I do like Spain; such cheap drink and the food's good. The place we stayed at did a great full English."

"It's in Italy," Martin pointed out. "Verona is in Italy."

"I'm thinking Valencia, still I bet Verona is good for a few beers."

Martin hoped that Sam Baxter's construction skills were superior to his geographical knowledge.

***

Later that morning, they once again visited Artemis at his home. They planned to share what they had learnt the previous day and then to ask him if he had any way of getting more information about Alan's last day before he either died or ran off into the sunset. But first Susan had an undiplomatic question for him. Although she never really understood the concept of undiplomatic.

"How come your hallway is half-painted, your kitchen has no door frame, or door for that matter. I presume it's the one leaning against your fridge freezer. Also, sitting here in your living room, it too appears to be mid-way through being decorated."

Artemis would like to have explained that each room was at a different stage of refurbishment. The hallway did have bright white paint around the front door and maybe three feet along one wall, it was a question of getting the right number of coats. He would say the hallway was in progress.

The front room was being prepared. Pictures removed from the walls, masking tape around the fireplace, light switches and electrical sockets loosened to allow cutting in of the paint just behind the plastic. Furniture moved towards the centre of the room, although not yet in a place where he could move his step ladders to paint the walls. The light shade was also removed.

The tins of paint remained unopened in the corner, along with brushes and rollers still wrapped in cellophane. The fabric dust sheet had been unpacked, then carefully refolded and laid over the decorating supplies to camouflage them. Preparation without a doubt.

The kitchen door was a little more complex. That had begun with a simple remove the door, make more space theory, which had worked. Artemis liked his kitchen without a door. It was just that the remaining door frame needed to be removed as well, which should have been an easy task. He began that project one Sunday afternoon while the Fidget pie he had made for dinner was in the oven. With hindsight he did not leave himself enough time. The first part of the architrave came away easily. The second part, when he managed to force it, took part of the frame, the wood splintered and took a large chunk of the plaster wall away with it.

At this point the pie was ready. Artemis left the door frame, or at least what was left of it, to have dinner. Nevertheless, he now deemed the kitchen door to be in a planning phase. Should he rip the frame out and replaster, and if that was the case, should he have an archway instead of a rectangle leading into the kitchen.

He decided that to answer Susan's valid question he had best keep things succinct. "My work leaves little time for DIY. How did the two of you get on yesterday?"

Susan recounted the places and people they had visited, something she was good at, Martin knew from experience.

He, on the other hand, often had trouble recalling conversations with people, which Susan was able to do almost verbatim. He attributed his inability to his low boredom threshold when people were talking to him. Often, he found his mind and thoughts wandering from listening to the person in front of him.

Artemis was unlike Martin. He listened intently to Susan, occasionally asking her a question, but overall allowing her to speak without interruption. He seemed pleased and highly satisfied with the information they had brought back.

"You think that Max Phillips is lying about the phone call. Do you have any idea why? There aren't any other connections to Alan as far as I can see."

"That's what we need to find out." Susan had wondered about it, but still felt sure she was right about the lying.

"Maybe he isn't lying. Possibly whoever Alan had planned to call after the wrong number, he changed his mind, who can tell?"

Artemis was offering an explanation that Susan thought implausible. She dismissed his view and asked him, "Have we any more information about the body?" She was hoping that they would at least have a name. No such luck.

"Nothing at all, I'm sorry to say. Police investigations continue, but I don't think they have our body as one of their priorities, unless we can prove it was a murder." Artemis shrugged, he knew how hard that might be, considering the cause of death was a heart attack. Maybe the only crime connected to the body was good old-fashioned body snatching.

"Well, I can see that I'll need to employ your services for a few more days. It's clearly worthwhile speaking to Mrs Hall again, ask her just who was in the car with her and touch on the possibility of her having an affair with her employer. If she truly believes her husband is dead, then she might admit her indiscretion.

"She might be able to point you in the right direction with the clothes, assuming the undertakers have returned them to her, especially that posh shirt the body was wearing. If the ambulance crew thought the shirt odd, it might help us to identify the body. It would seem we have a lot of questions for Mrs Hall. She, I think should be our focus from this point on. The best friend was only an observer and Mr Phillips seems to have been the victim of a misrouted telephone call. Mrs Hall is my person of interest."

Even though the room was prepared for decorating, alongside Artemis's high back chair, was a small coffee table with the TV remote, a glass of water and an opened bar of Cadbury's fruit and nut chocolate. The only other item was a picture frame showing a photograph of a small girl. Susan had noticed it the moment she had sat down. Could it be just a relation? Artemis wore no wedding ring and had never mentioned having a wife or partner.

"Who's the little girl?" Susan asked indicting the framed photograph, which Artemis immediately picked up and caressed in his hand.

"My daughter, Emily."

"I didn't realise you were married."

"Divorced, for a number of years now."

"Do you get to see her much?"

"No." he replaced the frame on the table with reverence. "She died not long after this photograph was taken. It was the tragedy of her death that pushed a wedge between my wife and I. But that's all in the past now.

"Let's focus on the present and our investigation. Do you have everything you need?"

"You said at the start of this, that you could help us with information that not everyone can access."

Artemis nodded positively, allowing Susan to continue. "It might help if we had his credit card records for a couple of weeks before his death. I guess you've already checked for any transactions after his death?"

"The first thing I did; nothing after the last day. Anything else that would help?"

"Double check his phone records, he had a reason to call someone at that time of night. Do you think Mrs Hall would let us examine his mobile phone, it might hold some clues."

"She might, but she can't. His mobile has never been located. Before you tell me the obvious, yes, it's odd and a little worrying, like most things in this case. I presume you'll be visiting the pub and speaking to the barmaids. Apart from that we have a brick wall approaching us, I fear."

Susan agreed on behalf of Hayden Investigations they would continue. At least she was confident Martin wouldn't mind asking a few questions where a pub was the venue.

"Oh, before you leave, there's one piece of information that I have only just been made aware of. The car, well the car Mrs Hall drives to be more precise, is not hers. The registered owner and keeper is the plumbing firm where she works. It's not uncommon for employees to have company cars but given the snippet of gossip you have brought me and the fact her job is office based, it might be something you might like to consider when talking to her." Artemis smiled.

***

As Martin was driving back to Christine Hall's house, he was in a grumpy mood, that was obvious to Susan and she knew the reason why, but had no intention of starting the conversation, aware that he would do so soon enough.

Five minutes into the journey, Martin began, "Let me get this right, one more visit to Mrs Hall, one visit to a pub and then we are done. I can start thinking about our Italian holiday?"

"Maybe," Susan left the word hanging in the air, making it sound like a threat. "Unless we uncover new lines of investigation, then we might need to do some more work. Don't forget, he's paying us, and not with peanuts either."

"Why bother, we don't need the money, do we? That was the whole purpose of my setting up Hayden Investigations, I never intended it to have any clients, paying or otherwise."

"Don't need the money? Did you see your credit card bill last month?"

He had seen it, thought it about normal, paid it in full and that was the end of it until the next month's credit card statement when the same procedure would happen. Susan, his now wife, had also seen it and been shocked. She thought her credit card bills before her marriage were high, but Martin's, well, he took expenditure to a whole other level.

"I paid it off," he commented.

Susan had more to say on the subject. "I know people who earn less in a month than you spend on luxuries in that time."

"I would not describe what I spend on my credit card as luxuries. There are household costs, petrol, social dining, plus that dress I bought you, the one you wore to the Wydhams."

"Not to mention," Susan was quick to point out, "the many Ubers you now take. A hundred pounds just to go from home to a London restaurant, when you could take the train. It might cost you twenty pounds return, whereas you spend two hundred pounds using Ubers. That is plain wasteful, I would say disgraceful."

Martin was not going to accept that anything he did was extravagant or wasteful. All his expenditure he considered to be practical and sensible. It was just how to relay that message to Susan. Shift the blame, always a good start, he thought.

"It was you who introduced me to Ubers and you who suggested that we live out of London. If I need a decent restaurant, I require the choice that London offers, not some mediocre restaurant in Highfield. Also, I'm avoiding the congestion charge by not taking my car, although I'm unlikely to take it as I would, without a doubt, have a drink."

"Take a train. Highfield station direct to Victoria, it doesn't get much easier or cheaper than that."

Okay, so the blame game and the practical sensible approach did not gain the traction he had hoped. There was another way: convenience.

"The train, I'd need to get a taxi to the station because I might be drinking. Then I'd have to time the taxi to collect me to coincide with the arrival of the train. The reverse of that late at night, becomes a lot more complex. An Uber picks you up at a time you require, takes you from one location to another and is equally efficient and convenient."

Martin would have liked to say, I now rest my case, but thought that might be going a step too far, so he just allowed Susan to digest his argument.

"You forgot wildly expensive. We're talking two hundred pounds just for your travel without the cost of the meal and your drinks. You might well spend over four hundred pounds in one night on one meal. Don't you know Martin, people earn less than that for a forty-hour week.

"If you keep on then I suggest we do some real paid work. At least that way you won't be frittering away your family fortune. Next time I'll drive you to the station and you can take a train."

Part of Martin wanted to continue this discussion, bringing into his argument the poor timekeeping of trains, the condition of the ancient rolling stock. Cold trains, which were dirty and unclean, with worn-out seats that made you cringe when you sat on them. Not that he had been on many trains since he left boarding school, but he had read about the problems train travellers face. But these facts could wait for another day. Martin had another idea, the next time Susan and he went out for lunch or a meal, he would ensure they ate frugally.

Chapter 11

Today, Christine warmly invited them into the PVC structure bolted onto the rear of her house, taking up about a third of the mainly grassed garden. She referred to it as a conservatory, as though it was something only the middle classes would enjoy. Neither Susan nor Martin was impressed. It was furnished to give the notion of being a tropical hot house.

"You must understand that any insurance claim would be handled by the company. As I wasn't driving at the time, I would be the last to hear of one."

"The thing is a man was reported driving the car on that day. We just wanted to know who it might be," Martin suggested, holding back on the CCTV evidence, wondering if she might deny being in the car at the time.

"It wasn't my husband driving if that's what you're thinking, even you know it was after his death. But I can see where your minds might be going. My husband is dead, of that, I'm sure."

"That might be so, but it would help us if we knew who was driving that day," Martin was pushing her for the name of the driver.

If they expected her to lie, they were wrong.

Yes, she was in the car that day with another man, her boss, the owner of the plumbing firm where she worked and the registered owner of the car. She volunteered the information without being pushed, which Susan thought odd. Christine had gone into Tesco to pick up supplies.

When she returned to the car, her boss told her that a woman had bumped into it.

She paused before continuing, "I never gave it another thought after that, the bump, as he described it. If you're wondering, he drove my car because my mind was still all over the place, it was soon after Alan's death. That was the reason he drove me to the shop to pick up tea, coffee and snacks for the office."

"There wasn't any other explanation for you being with your boss in the car shopping?" Susan said, although she would have liked to have added, 'Is this the boss everyone thinks you're knocking off,' but thought that a bit too blunt.

"No, maybe he thought getting away from the office might be beneficial to me. I don't know. He suggested restocking the tea cupboard, then said he'd drive me. There was no other reason. You must understand, that my boss, or Manny to those who know him well, is a good friend and employer, everyone likes him. Manny has seen what I have been going through over the last few weeks and has shown me true compassion and sympathy. It's called being a good human being."

Susan drew back from her line of questioning. If she was hoping to get a confession, then she was mistaken. Sharon had only hinted that Christine might be having an affair, maybe it was with someone else. Susan thought it best to change the subject.

"Last time we were here you mentioned he was buried in his brown suit. Did you get the clothes he was wearing when he died from the undertaker?" Susan asked.

"No. The undertakers offered them back when they came to collect the brown suit, but what use would I have with them? I guess they still have the clothes."

Martin had only been semi-listening to the conversation while thinking about putting a conservatory on the side of their house. It could be useful in the cooler months of spring and autumn. He would leave a final decision until the kitchen was completed and operational. For now, he chose to enter the discussion.

"Did your husband have any diversions, outside interests? I know he liked his bikes. Anything else he might have been interested in?"

"I'm sure he had lots of diversions; he was a bloke after all. The one I knew about was his bikes. Well, he called it an interest, it was more just imitating his mate, Bill at work. That's why he bought his old bike readymade, unlike Bill, building them almost from scratch. Even so, that old bike was his pride and joy, luckily it was his other bike that got stolen."

"His bike got stolen?" Martin queried.

"About a month before he died. As I say, not the old one he rode around the countryside with his mates, it was a simple modern bike that was stolen. He always used it for work, flying past the traffic, it was economical as well. But one night he was filling it up and someone took it off the station forecourt. When it got stolen, Alan was grumpy as hell and acted like a bear with a sore head."

Susan, wearing a deep frown, looked at Martin. She turned back to Mrs Hall.

"Did he make an insurance claim?"

"Yes, but even getting paid out didn't improve his mood."

"Just one last thing," Susan changed tack to a previous subject she wanted an answer to, the other man that might be in Christine's life. "Who was the friend you stayed with soon after Alan had died? You appeared to imply it was not the one in Crawley."

If looks could kill, Christine's eyes would have needed a licence, and Susan would be sprawled on the floor dead.

"I can't see what that has to do with an insurance claim for my husband's life. My arrangements following his death have no bearing on the claim, that I assume you're trying to establish is either false or legitimate. Unless you believe that I'm in some way part of a scam and my husband is alive and trying to defraud your company. If that's the case, then you'd better make some serious allegations. And before you do, you're no one important, you aren't the police. I don't need to tell you anything at all," Christine spat the words out with venom.

"The friend, the one you stayed with, was it Manny?" Susan liked the occasional spat. Martin was wondering if he was going to have to part the two warring women anytime soon. He did not need to worry.

"You'd better leave now; I'm telling you nothing because I have no reason to justify my actions to the two of you."

Martin and Susan left the warm conservatory without any protest. Susan knew that what Sharon had hinted at, Christine now had all but confirmed.

***

The Cross Swords public house was not on Sidcup High Street as Sharon had described. It laid back a little, along a small narrow street, positioned at the end of a row of small, terraced houses which made the free house look grand. It was symmetrical, with an open door on each side of two large windows draped with net curtains. In the centre, two wooden picnic tables, each with an ash tray and a Foster's umbrella, were wedged between the four steps that led up to the doors.

The upper exterior was decked in mock Tudor beams with green and gold signage, together with a line of four, equally spaced hanging flower baskets. Martin considered that the Cross Swords was a good example of a privately owned public house. The owner no doubt liked everything to be well laid out and balanced. There was nothing corporate about the pub. Martin wondered if that was the reason Alan had made this pub his regular haunt.

Inside, just a few minutes after morning opening time, there were already about six old men scattered around the small saloon, each had a pint of some description beside them, each was reading a tabloid, but for one man, sitting at a corner table, who was scanning the broadsheet pages of The Times.

Martin ordered a coffee. At least this establishment had succumbed to one of the better changes for those stuck with driving, selling teas and coffees as well as alcoholic drinks. Susan went for a large white wine; she had no plans to drive soon.

The landlord who served them was pleasant and welcoming to these new faces at the bar. The indifference the other drinkers displayed pointed to the fact that this pub was overall a good family local, not a drinking club for characters of dubious backgrounds.

As Martin paid, he began to explain the reason for their visit, asking about Alan Hall who recently died. The landlord smiled, but before he had a chance to answer another voice spoke up.

"That's the old bugger who fell out of the coffin," the Times reader quickly put in his point of view. He had approached the bar unseen for a refill.

"His coffin, not his body," the landlord corrected with a smirk. Without being asked, he took the empty glass from the Times man and pulled him another pint of Doom Bar.

"Has he fled the country, started a new life?" asked Times newspaper man.

"That's what we're trying to establish, it would seem unlikely that his body has been mislaid. We're here looking to see if we can get any clues as to his whereabouts. Was he a regular?"

"Not as regular as Jim here," the landlord with a grin nodded towards the Times man. "But Alan was in at least once a week, mainly in the morning as he worked nights, but I guess you already knew that. Haven't seen him since his death or disappearance, whatever you fancy calling it."

Ignoring the stupidity of the last remark, Martin enquired if Alan drank alone, or socialised with the regulars.

"Well, he often drank with another guy, Ian, I think his name was." The bearded landlord picked up some glasses and started to wipe them with a grey cloth, bringing up the shine in each of them. "I know he had a wife, he mentioned her a few times, but in the main him and his mate chatted. When they did include me, it was about football or motor racing. Alan was a Ferrari fan I recall that."

"What about the other thing?" Times newspaper man asked, making the landlord look uncomfortable.

"What other thing?" Susan pounced on the question. This did not sound bland or banal.

"Nowt to do with us." The landlord liked to be as discreet as he could about the habits of his customers.

"Maybe not, but we all suspected. True or false?" Times man was now talking as if he was in a cryptic crossword.

The landlord looked down the bar towards a young woman who was busy wrapping knives and forks in napkins, preparing for the lunchtime rush of food orders.

"Ask Pepsi, she might know more about Alan than us blokes." The inference was apparent to Susan and Martin. Maybe she was the diversion Mrs Hall had talked about.

As the Hayden team introduced themselves to the barmaid, she at once pointed out that her name was Nicola, she would prefer they used that and not Pepsi. She seemed uptight, at having been pointed out as a friend of Alan. She had long brown crinkly hair that draped down over her shoulders. Her rounded face and bright eyes gave her a look of fun-loving attractiveness, which maybe on a better day she might be. Today she was being tedious.

"Did they send you over?"

"They suggested we speak to you about Alan. They said you might know a bit more about him," Susan asked the question, hoping to soothe the barmaid.

"First off, whatever they've told you, I wasn't knocking him off. Just because I went out with him a couple of times, their dirty minds think I dropped my knickers, I didn't. He was too old and too married."

"But you went out with him?" Susan wanted confirmation.

Her defences appeared raised to the point that Susan considered she was not going to get anything out of her. Susan need not have worried, appearances could be deceptive, Nicola liked to talk.

"Why not? We chatted when he was in here, we both like Turkey. The country place not the feathered bird you eat at Christmas. He'd been there with his wife, and I'd been as well, different part, with my ex-boyfriend. We talked about the place; you know holiday stuff. General chit-chat at the bar, that was all. He said he knew this good Turkish restaurant and we should go there one day, relive our holiday, as he put it."

"Just the once?"

She stopped wrapping the cutlery in napkins. It seemed to Martin multi-tasking was not one of her strong points.

"We went a couple of times, just chatted and had a laugh. It was better than going out with a younger bloke who would have had his hands all over me."

"Alan didn't try anything on?"

"Who Alan?! No, a real gent. Always paid for the meal. Told me he enjoyed my company, which is more than a lot of the regulars here want, I can tell you. They might be old, but their eyes still gawk at me." She looked over at the eyes that she could feel looking her way from the other end of the bar.

"Where's this place Alan took you?"

"The Rich Sultan. It's in Barnehurst, on the high street. He was a regular there, the first time we walked in it was all, 'Hello Alan, normal table'. Felt like royalty when I ate in there with him, I can tell you. Good food, just like Turkey, even had Efes beer. Shame him dying and that."

"That?"

"Falling out the coffin and not being him; weird, don't you think?"

"I do think it weird," Susan nodded in agreement. "Did he ever talk to you about any future plans, dreams, hopes? Anything you might think odd."

Nicola stopped and screwed her face up as she thought about the question. Clearly, Martin judged, Susan had given her too many alternatives in one sentence. She should have kept it simpler for her. Patiently they waited.

"Only the twenty quid he dropped, that was weird," she stopped speaking. Martin encouraged her to share more details, which she then freely did.

"This bloke came up to our table, said Alan must have dropped a twenty-pound note in the toilet. The bloke had, as I understand it, gone in after Alan. The gents were the same as the ladies, just the one cubicle. None of that peeing-up-the-wall thing for the blokes. Alan didn't seem sure at first but took the bank note and thanked him. Well, I would have taken it if I'd dropped it or not. He said it must have fallen out of his trousers, I thought it was really honest of the bloke, I'd have kept the money if I'd found it on the floor, toilet or not."

"I guess Alan had just come back?"

"Ah yes, he went while we were waiting for our desserts. That's the thing with drinking beer, makes you pee a lot, the bubbles, he said."

"And that was all there was between you and Alan, a friend's lunch?" Susan asked not believing the barmaid. Martin was a little more compassionate.

"Yeah, I told you nothing else, just a meal. He was married you know. I know what those over there think, but I'm not that type," she added with a defensive voice looking over towards the regulars. "They'd like me to be, but I'm not."

As Susan and Martin walked back to the car, they did not speak but had the same thought. They tried to imagine a situation where someone could drop a bank note when going to the toilet. It was not impossible, but certainly not likely. That led them to wonder if it was a real twenty-pound note, or something else the 'bloke', as Nicola had described him, had given Alan. Could he have been a contact Alan was making at the restaurant. He was, after all, by Nicola's reckoning, a regular at the venue. It had to be worth a visit. Sitting in the car Susan Googled the restaurant; it had an interesting menu.

"Looks like we're having Turkish for lunch," Susan indicated, as she entered the address in the sat nav.

Chapter 12

As set-price lunchtime menus go, the one that Martin was looking through made his mouth water. The Rich Sultan offered a good range of food on its two-course lunchtime menu which made choosing a little difficult. After much deliberation and rebuffing the waiter on three occasions, Martin made a choice: Saksuka, - deep-fried aubergine cubes cooked in a special tomato sauce with onion, pepper & garlic - followed by Chicken Beyti, described as spicy marinated minced chicken seasoned with garlic, chargrilled, served with rice and salad. He asked for a jug of tap water, he was driving. Susan took a plainer approach, grilled sea bass with chips, she emphasised the chips and not salad or rice. Plus, a large glass of white wine, for Susan this was becoming a fun day.

The restaurant was decked out in a plain, yet luxurious décor. There was however a gaudy-looking neon sign in the far corner, which seemed to be out of place. It was, for Martin, the food that was the overriding factor of any dining establishment. Being a lunchtime, Martin thought it was well-supported, with at least a third of all the tables having at least one diner seated. As he finished his Chicken Beyti, he could understand why Alan visited this place regularly.

Susan said the fish was okay, but the waiter ignored her opinion as he removed their plates. She took the opportunity to order another large glass of wine.

When the chilled glass was placed in front of her, she showed the waiter the photograph Artemis had given her at the start of the case.

The waiter looked at it. It might not have been the best portrait of Alan, but it was the only one Susan had been given. The waiter was not sure if he had ever seen him in the restaurant. When Martin added that Alan usually came in during the day, the waiter acknowledged that he was normally on the evening shift and pointed to Deniz who was always on the day shift so might be able to help them.

"I didn't know you had a picture of Alan," Martin said as he took the photograph and examined the features.

"Artemis gave it to me. Haven't needed it so far, but it's handy, it's what we detectives do best, have evidence to hand," Susan smiled. "How else would you have thought that I would recognise Alan when I was viewing shoppers going into Tesco."

It turned out that Deniz was the manager, who beamed when he saw the photograph.

"Yes, Alan, Tuesday Alan. Not seen him in a while, is everything okay?" Deniz grinned, revealing a set of teeth that were just too white to be natural, they emphasised his dusky skin.

"He's missing," Martin replied, deciding that was the easiest and most precise description he could give of Alan's status. If he was dead, he was missing. If Alan was alive, he was still missing. In addition, it avoided a long story about the bizarre circumstances that had led to him not being accounted for.

"Run off with his girl!" Deniz scoffed.

"Maybe, did he have one?" Martin asked coolly as he wondered if Nicola was telling the whole truth.

"Only saw him once, or I think maybe twice, with a young girl, holding hands and kissing, not his wife, I guarantee. If she's gone too, then there you have it, Romeo and Juliet."

"Every Tuesday you say?" Martin wanted to ignore the girl, she was still stuck working in the Cross Swords bored out of her mind and not on some Turkish beach with Alan. Unless perhaps there was another woman in the frame that they had yet to hear about.

"Yeah. Mid-afternoon he'd come in with the girl, sometimes with a guy, but mostly on his own. Had his two-course lunch, a couple of beers, little chat maybe if he was on his own, then off he went."

"The guy who he came in with, can you describe him?"

"Shortish guy, thin, black hair with a beard, his beard was more grey than black."

That sounded to them like Ian Cook, the best friend, which would make sense. Taking a friend to have lunch with, nothing sinister in that. Was this going to be a dead end? Nicola could not recall what the man who handed Alan the twenty-pound note looked like, apart from the fact he was old, which in the circumstances was not a lot of help. They could not really ask for a list of honest customers, that would be pointless, and staff would not know for certain.

Deniz, having misinterpreted why he was needed at the table, stood holding the credit card machine having placed the bill on the table.

Martin, thinking there was not much more to get from the restaurant, handed over his credit card, which sparked a thought.

"How did he pay?"

"Who, Alan? Cash always. Not many pay cash nowadays, most are on the cards, but Alan never used one."

What that meant to Martin, he was not sure. He felt he was grasping at straws, every lead he followed ending in a cul-de-sac. There was nothing obvious, nothing to cry out Alan had run off with a woman, man, or a bag of cash. Nothing.

Susan, having watched numerous television detectives go about their fictional work, immediately thought Alan didn't want to be traced to this restaurant, he was covering his tracks. She thought it significant.

"Is that what's 'is name?" The question was asked by a short waiter who was clearing the table a little too quickly, Martin thought. He might have the same skin complexion as Deniz, but he didn't earn enough for tooth veneers, even though it would have helped his public image as he had such yellowed teeth.

As Martin and Susan listened, it became clear that the short waiter had noticed Alan had not been in for a few weeks, he seemed to be honestly concerned Alan was missing. It was not unusual for table waiters to offer their own version of circumstances of their customer's lives. Short waiter was no exception and gave his own thoughts about the current situation.

"Run off with Asian Adana; we haven't seen him in a while either."

"Don't be so stupid, he wasn't like that," Deniz reprimanded the waiter for suggesting such a thing. "You saw what he was like with his woman."

"Who's Asian Adana?" Martin asked, the name Adana seemed familiar to him, where or how he could not quite place. He scoured his memory, then it popped up, Adana Kebab, the first lamb dish on the restaurant menu.

Short waiter answered, after all it was only his theory, however wild his boss thought it might be.

"Asian Adana comes in every Tuesday as well, normally arrives about a half hour before Alan. The Asian always has the Adana Kebab, not with chips, nor the rice and salad, didn't want that, he wanted steamed aubergines. We'd walk into the kitchen, call out Asian Adana, then we'd get the kebabs with aubergines. Everyone knew the dish. But he's not been around for a while and certainly not since Alan has gone missing. See, told you, they've run off together."

"Did they ever speak to each other?"

"No, it was only because he and Alan were regulars that you got to expect them. Alan was always chatty and friendly, Adana kept himself to himself, never found out his real name."

"And always paid cash." It was as if Deniz, who kept an eye on all the financial transactions, had read Susan's mind. Like her, he was a fan of TV detectives.

Susan asked what this quiet Asian guy looked like. Short waiter again took up the task, having served him a number of times, he recalled him easily.

"Well, he was tall, but there again most people are taller than me. But he was taller than most Indians are, if he was Indian. He looked as if he came from that part of the world. Thin face, slim build, always looked bored and fed up. Also had a funny hand, well I say funny, he was missing a thumb. Would love to have asked how he lost it, but he was never that approachable."

Susan felt they had just unlocked a door. Now there was a coincidence, a tall, thin Asian man, with a missing thumb, just like the guy at the old man's house. There had to be a connection, it was just too much of a chance that Alan's last call was to the house where the Asian man just happened to go to the same diner, on the same day and at almost the same time.

"This might seem like an odd question, but did the Asian ever use the toilet?"

"Yes, I think so, but never together." Deniz was quick to make it clear he would not allow anything like that in his establishment.

"No, but funny you should ask that," the short waiter recalled. "Asian Adana would always go to the loo first, then very soon after, Alan would go. Never did I see Alan go before Asian Adana. I notice odd things about customers."

Martin would have used the facilities before he left anyway. That was only sensible. His mother had always told him, 'Best go for a wee before we leave the house, can't have you being caught short'. It was a habit he had never grown out of.

Susan did ask if she could come with him, but all Deniz said was that there is a separate water closet for ladies. Martin smiled and left Susan at the table.

Just as Nicola had described – how she knew Martin did not want to speculate – the men's was no more than a single cubicle with a toilet, a wash basin and a hand dryer. The whole room was finished off in black glossy marble-effect tiles, which made the small room feel even smaller.

Martin stood and looked around. He just felt there had to be a sign or something about this room. The only time the paths of Alan and the Asian would have crossed was in this area, albeit not at the same time. Was there a reason they were both here on the same day?

Again, Martin looked at every item in the room. The toilet brush, the rolls of toilet paper stacked on the cistern. The anti-bacterial handwash on the sink, the mirror, nice and clean. The drawer below the sink. He recalled Susan and Colin once saying they always look in bathroom cabinets when they are in someone else's house, a habit that Martin had never considered before, believing it to be an invasion of privacy. But the drawer tempted him. He was after all investigating a case and it was not as if it was a private toilet, he was not a guest in someone's house, he was a customer.

Martin pulled out the drawer. Extra toilet rolls, a pair of yellow rubber gloves a container of toilet gel, a screwdriver and two additional bottles of handwash.

But the drawer seemed not deep enough for the depth of the basin. On a whim he pulled it out completely and put it on the floor, nothing behind it at all, just an empty void. He bent down to return the drawer to its rightful place when he noticed something. Discarded and serving no apparent purpose, a strip of masking tape was stuck to the back of the drawer. It looked fresh, not dried out, it was not debris left over from when the sink unit was originally installed.

Did it have a purpose or was Martin getting to be a little too like Susan, grasping at the slightest thing that might be a clue.

He took a twenty-pound note out of his wallet, placed it against the back of the drawer, it fitted with ease. He could tape the bank note and close the drawer, there was a good-sized void once it was back in place. Enough space, Martin calculated, for a wad of notes, a wad of twenty-pound notes. One of which Alan might have dropped after collecting the money, only to have it returned by an honest diner.

This room was a collection point. The Asian man could be delivering cash for Alan to gather. The question was, what was the Asian man paying for?

***

Barry Gladstone was less than amused to see Susan walk into the reception area. She had again come in alone, leaving Martin in the car babbling on about not wanting to see dead bodies. He was at times a total wimp, she decided.

"I hope this won't take long," Barry sounded anxious. "I have a funeral leaving in five minutes, so you have a little less than that. What do you want now?"

Susan made her request for the clothes that Alan was wearing when he was picked up. It might have been simple in Susan's mind, but not for Barry. He huffed and puffed, then hollered loudly, "Graham, get here!"

A short, rotund teenager with a little too much acne on his long face, appeared from an alcove behind the reception. He looked timidly at Barry, he seemed fearful of what he might be needed for.

"Graham, look after this lady," he barked. "She wants to see the clothes that Alan Hall was wearing when we picked him up. They'll be in the charity cupboard, give her what she wants. Then while we're gone, clear up that bloody mess of dead flowers in the loading dock before they start rotting and change into a compost heap."

He turned back to Susan. "He'll look after you. I'm off now." Without any pleasantries he walked out of the building to join a hearse and two limousines parked outside.

Graham looked at Susan, decided that she was good-looking, and promptly felt his cheeks redden with embarrassment, before he said, "Best follow me."

Susan followed him through a maze of corridors, two odd-shaped rooms, the first of which resembled a shed with multiple tools and boxes filling the space. The second one had a variety of coffin parts, odd lids, some sides, bags and bags of handles as well as a number of small wooden caskets. She decided not to ask for an explanation of anything she had seen. She did, once they arrived at the charity cupboard, have the urge to query what the cupboard was about, but decided against it, assuming that the clue was in the name.

More of a walk-in wardrobe, she stood in the doorway while Graham began moving boxes around.

"What was his last name?" He obviously was not the most attentive listener.

"Hall, Alan Hall," Susan confirmed as Graham reached up to a shelf and pulled down a brown cardboard box, which carried the branding of a famous pasta company.

"You look incredibly young to be working as an undertaker," Susan pointed out, realising that Graham, apart from being short and fat, looked as if shaving was something he had not yet grown into, his skin was pale and smooth. He reddened again.

"I'm on work experience."

He took off the lid and began to sort through the plastic bags that were packed into the box.

"I would have thought this a strange choice for work experience, being with the dead. Do you want to be an undertaker when you leave school?"

"God forbid. Working with dead bodies is bad enough. Working with people who enjoy working with dead bodies is even worse."

"Then why choose it for work experience?"

"It's complicated, it wouldn't interest you."

"Try me," was the challenge Susan laid down for him.

"Next door to this place is a solicitor's office," Graham paused.

"Yes, I saw it as I walked in. What's it got to do with your work experience?"

"Sandra Fuller's doing her work experience there. She's one of the best-looking girls in the class. Well, we get to hang out together for lunch. Every day, I get her all to myself. Now working amongst all these dead bodies, I'm wondering if she's worth it."

"I'm sure she is, Graham. The path of true love is never smooth. I'm positive she recognises your self-sacrifice to be with her."

"Do you really think so?" His eyes lit up, was he truly getting approval for his plan from a good-looking, older lady.

"I'm sure." She wanted to ignore the question, not wishing to offer any romantic advice to a lovelorn teenager, after all, she was not the best person to do so. "Are they the clothes?"

"Oh, yes." His thoughts were elsewhere as he handed the plastic bag to Susan.

It was then Susan realised, apart from a very bored-looking middle-aged receptionist, there was only Graham at the undertakers. Everyone else appeared to be out on a funeral. She had a plan, a thought about a way to see if any of the dead bodies that were hanging around the undertakers at the time of Alan's arrival were all present and correct.

"Graham, when people visit the Chapel of Rest to see their loved ones, is there a record kept of them?"

"Yeah, they kind of sign in. Do you want to see it?"

Susan did and she followed him from the charity cupboard clutching the plastic bag of clothes. Then after a few doors and a couple of corridors, they were standing at the entrance to the Chapel of Rest. He picked up a book from a table that was set beside the door with a tiny posy of plastic flowers in an equally plastic vase.

Susan checked the date of Alan's arrival at the undertakers and the date of the funeral, then examined the entries between those dates. Graham helpfully pointed out that the deceased name was first and the visitor was named alongside it together with the date they visited.

Susan's logic was if every other dead body was viewed in the Chapel of Rest by a relative, or at least a person who knew them, then all the bodies were correctly identified. Meaning that the last body, Alan's, never arrived at the undertakers.

It is often the unexpected that puts everything into confusion. The surprise was according to this book, the body of Alan Hall was laid out in the Chapel of Rest and received a visitor three days before the funeral. That to Susan made little sense. Someone who knew Alan, paid their respects to the body, so it must have been Alan lying dead in the chapel after all. But that she could not believe unless she was wrong about Ian lying.

The other thing Susan had not expected was the arrival of another Gladstone employee, a young man dressed in a neatly tailored morning suit.

"What's going on here?" he demanded, clearly not happy about seeing a stranger with the work experience boy, who had been an irritant ever since his arrival.

"Mr Gladstone said she could do what she likes."

"Did he?" The newly arrived employee did not think his boss was that generous.

"I think the phrase was," Susan recalled, "give her what she wants."

"Graham, you go off to lunch, I've just seen your girlfriend wander down the road."

Graham scuttled quickly away without a further word.

"I'm Pete. It's about the missing body, isn't it; it's the only bloody subject of conversation these days. I'm convinced we will soon be besieged by murderers asking for us to lose bodies. What are you after exactly?"

"I think I might have found it. Alan Hall, the missing body, had a visitor in the chapel."

"Yes, I oversaw it, and I told old man Gladstone someone came and saw the bloody body, so it must have been the right one."

"You were here when the visitor viewed the body?"

Pete did not like to admit it. He was a very cagey person; some would say shifty. Once he knew that Susan was an investigator, he wondered just how much he should admit. This was not going away, maybe a bit of horse-trading might help him in the long term.

"Yeah. A bloke turned up, I think he was old, well, he had a big overcoat on, a flat cap and dark glasses, said his eyes were sensitive. Walked with a limp. Spent no more than five minutes and then left. Nothing much more to say about it. Sometimes people spend an hour or more with their loved ones, other times a few minutes, everyone mourns in different ways."

"Could the visitor have taken the missing tools, you know the ones in the coffin that the deceased requested?"

Pete took a deep breath. "They never ended up in the coffin, they were a nice set of tools. I pocketed them, well, if it wasn't going to be me, the blokes at the crematorium would have had them away. Does it make any difference, I mean, no harm done. As a favour, can it be between you and me?" It was more of a plea than a request.

Susan laughed. "Any job always has an incentive to be had somewhere. Anything else about this missing body I should know?"

"What, apart from being the wrong body, you mean," he laughed, feeling that Susan was not overly worried about his thieving. "The suit, the brown suit the widow wanted him buried in, bit on the large size for him, but not all clothes fit perfectly either in life or death. The thing was, in the pocket there was a bunch of keys, well, I say bunch, three keys on a boring plastic fob, but there was also a nice-looking Ferrari one. I was going to ask the widow if they should be there, but I thought it was part of the deal. People do funny things for dead relatives. Plus, the fob, not the plastic one, I did take a liking to, a genuine Ferrari, I was sure."

"But what happened?" Susan sensed there was something more than him just nicking the key fob.

"I left them in there, in the suit pocket planning to, shall we say, lose the keys and the fob just before I nailed down the coffin. When the time came, I dug around his pocket, they weren't there."

"You think the visitor?" Susan consulted the visitors' book to note the name.

"I'd put money on it."

***

"It's almost five o'clock. Isn't that a bit late to start work on the kitchen?" Martin asked as he arrived home with Susan who was clutching a plastic bag of clothes. On the drive was a large sign-written transit van with Sam and his mate unloading a selection of tools and equipment.

"Never too late to start," Sam laughed as he clung onto a large tool chest. "Thought we'd get some of our kit in ready for an early start in the morning."

"What do you call an early start?" Martin asked, fully aware that the term early start has several definitions depending on just who is saying it. For an office cleaner, it could be 5am. A waiter might consider 11am an early start. A night shift worker, such as the late Alan Hall, his early start could be 5pm.

"About seven, but we won't be making much noise 'til about eight, better for the neighbours. You can get some right grumpy ones I can tell you."

"Wouldn't it then be better to start at eight, or even a bit later."

"No, but we do finish about three in the afternoon. Early start, early finish."

"I appreciate that, but..." Martin wondered how easy it might be to negotiate a later start which would suit him far better. "Couldn't you start, say at nine, make noise straight away and then finish at about five?"

"Doesn't work in our trade. If we start at nine, then do two hours and stop for breakfast, drops us right in the middle of lunch. Much better to start at seven, breakfast at nine, then on the way back from the cafe, pop into the wholesalers and pick up what we need for that day. It works a dream, don't it, Kenny?" Sam looked at his mate, who just nodded and smiled.

Martin, with a look of resignation, walked into the house with Susan behind him. He could tell she was smiling, it was in her voice, "Shall I set your alarm?"

Chapter 13

Susan cautiously unpacked the clothes that had been removed from the dead body, previously known as Alan Hall when it arrived at Gladstone Undertakers. Having spoken to the ambulance crew about the upmarket unusual label on the polo shirt, it was the sole focus in her mind. What she hadn't considered, now much to her regret, was that the shirt was not the only item the body had worn. Also, what happens to a body once the final breath is taken.

That was the reason that she was now out in the garden where Martin had banished her, gingerly taking out each item, before laying it on the grass in two piles. In pile one were the items she was not going to look at in any detail, they would go straight back into the plastic bag. Pile two were the items which she had more interest in: the polo shirt, a jean jacket and a pair of soiled chinos, which once she had checked the pockets would join pile one.

Martin had insisted she open the plastic bag in the middle of the lawn, well away from the house. He remained steadfastly on the decking, drinking a coffee. He had no plans to go anywhere near her or the clothes.

"You could help," she called from the centre of the lawn, on her knees.

"They've all been checked, there's nothing to find. Just look at the Devred 1902 label on the polo shirt," Martin called out.

Maybe it was a step too far. If she had mulled over the idea of checking the clothes, she might have realised there would be underclothes as well as outer clothes. Still, she wasn't going to give up now. Even though the polo shirt, with its French label had no pockets, the chinos did, but they produced nothing except an unpleasant stench. The denim jacket was whiffy, having been trapped in the airtight plastic bag for the last few weeks, but the smell was not totally overpowering. It had pockets, one on each breast. The first one was empty, as was the second, or did she feel something? Susan rummaged a bit more; the thin latex gloves were not the best to search with, but they were a necessity. There was something. She pulled out a tightly folded till receipt just like the ones you get in supermarkets.

"Ah!" she yelled with a resonance of triumph, "a clue."

"Probably a used tissue," Martin ridiculed her discovery, even though he had no idea what she had in her hand.

Carefully she unfolded it. It was a supermarket receipt, just not any company she had ever heard of. Susan stood up and walked towards Martin, waving the till receipt in front of her. "The bloke had been shopping at 'U'," she said as she sat down next to Martin and tried to hand it to him. He rebuffed her offer.

"I'm not touching it."

"Death isn't contagious," she pointed out, trying to get him to take the strip of flimsy paper.

"If that thing is full of germs, then death could certainly be the outcome. Read it out."

Susan tried but didn't recognise the words on the bill, apart from the large 'U' which she guessed must be the shop brand. She looked down the list of items, unable to decipher what the unknown man had bought during the last days of his life. Upon a closer inspection, she began to understand. Poire, she recalled from her school days. Blanc, well that was French for white, she knew that from drinking wine. Quiche Lorraine, also French, or at least came from France. She pulled the receipt tight and displayed it to Martin. "I think it's French."

From a safe distance, yet still in visual range, Martin read the receipt. She was right, he recognised the logo; it was a French store he had seen on a recent trip with a coach full of pensioners. He looked down the list, wine, food, a bit of fruit. He then looked at the location, ZAC de Ker d'Hervé, Loudeac,22600, FR.

"Yes, you're right, Sherlock, a French supermarket receipt. Even more interesting is that the date is the morning of Alan's presumed death." He looked into Susan's eyes and grinned broadly. "I think you might have a vital clue in your hand."

"We're all done for the night."

Sam had joined them, his shorts out of place with the large steel-capped boots he was wearing. He looked at the small pile of clothes on the lawn and the plastic bag next to it. Then to Susan who was still wearing the blue latex gloves and holding a small till receipt. "Forensics, eh? Gotta love a bit of forensics action. Do you watch that CSI bloke? Cracking little TV show, never knew flies could tell you so much. What we got here then?"

Happy to give him a closer look at her latest clue, Sam nodded as Susan told him about the clothes and finding the receipt deep in one of the pockets. Their kitchen fitter seemed impressed that the pile of clothes was from a dead man, he was still more fascinated with his new clients' activities. His excitement level dulled as Susan told him that it was about the wrong body falling out of the coffin, he must have heard about it on the news.

"Can't say I have," he admitted sheepishly. "Don't get much time for the news and stuff, but it does sound a pretty weird story. Anyway, we're off now. Back in the morning and we'll be cracking on. Have a good night."

He turned and walked back through the side gate, out to his van. He hoped they hadn't noticed the large scrape along the driver's side. Maybe he should get it fixed or at the very least hire a different one for the next couple of weeks. Small world, he thought, he had not only heard of the body falling out of the coffin, but he was also there at the time; something he planned to keep to himself.

***

Only after Susan had put the clothes back in the plastic bag, tied the top as tightly as possible, then stashed it in the small garden shed at the bottom of the garden behind a substantial buddleia bush, was she allowed back into the house. Then she showered thoroughly before joining Martin in the living room. It was now time to make sense of the last couple of days.

The body, which Susan had christened Pierre, appeared to have done his shopping in the morning at a supermarket in the middle of Brittany, France. By that evening he lay dead in Alan Hall's workshop. It didn't take a huge leap of faith to connect this apparent time travel to Potts Field airport. Pierre, they thought, must have flown into Potts Field during the day, either as a passenger or a pilot.

It was easy to agree that anyone can have a heart attack, which is what must have happened to poor Pierre. What neither Martin or Susan could understand was why Ian and, no doubt Alan, took it upon themselves to move the body to the workshop before palming the dead Frenchman off as one of them. Why not just call the ambulance and police, like most normal citizens would? Unless, of course, they had something to hide, but what?

Then there was the wife, Christine, did she have any connection to the dead man? Plus, she mentioned the bike being stolen, whereas Artemis had only told them about the car collision. And was it possible her suspected affair was connected to the death?

Not forgetting the Indian man lacking a thumb. He was at Max Phillip's house, where Alan had made his last call. Then Alan and the Indian chap dined on the same day at the same restaurant, a place where there was possibly a transaction of cash. From whom and to whom, they could not be sure.

Lastly, if Pete, who Susan had described as a little untrustworthy, was telling the truth, a set of keys was missing. Keys that had probably been collected from Alan's brown suit, on the body of the Frenchman in the Chapel of Rest, by someone with a limp called Archie Nihill. A visitor who should have known that the body in the chapel was not Alan's.

"Drugs or perhaps contraband," was Susan's conclusion. Martin was not so sure.

"Let's not forget Alan and his work colleague have a common interest in motorbikes. We're only assuming that Pierre flew over. Maybe he brought a bike to the UK, possibly one that was highly valuable and possibly stolen. It happens a lot with high-value cars in the UK being sent abroad.

"Either way, in the first instance we should go and see Alan's best friend, now we know that it wasn't Alan on the floor. That nugget of information might well encourage him to speak. He no doubt knows more than he's letting on."

Susan was surprised at what she heard. Martin wanting to investigate? Something he had been trying to avoid over the last couple of days. He must have another reason.

"What's the catch? You wanting to dig deeper in this case?" Susan asked.

"Because it's preferable to going up the stairs and trying to translate a set of odd drawings, that should, but do not, help me construct that IKEA Billy corner unit of yours. I would much rather question Ian Cook."

"And count how many lies he tries to tell this time," Susan added.

Chapter 14

"Who is it?" Ian called through his locked front door in response to Martin loudly knocking the weathered and tarnished skull-shaped door knocker.

Martin had not paid much attention to the surroundings the last time he visited Ian, his mind had been firmly on preparing for Italy. A destination that appeared to be receding as this investigation seemed to be getting more complex by the minute.

For the first time Martin recognised that Ian lived in one of six terraced houses in this small cul-de-sac called Factory Road. Back when they were first built Martin guessed there would have been terraced houses along the length of the road, housing for the factory workers. The factory had long since gone, as had most of the other houses. The remaining six tired terraced homes appeared as if they had been placed in the middle of a brownfield site. Dereliction surrounded them and that would no doubt be their fate in time.

"It's Susan and Martin; we spoke the other day about Alan Hall."

"What do you want to know?"

"We have some more information and wanted to ask you a few questions."

There was a short silence before the sound of a bolt being pulled across and a key turning, then the Yale lock was released and the door was timidly opened.

Ian stood holding the door ajar just enough for Martin and Susan to squeeze into the house. As soon as they were inside, he closed the door, flipped the Yale lock, and used the mortice lock to further secure it.

"Can't be too careful nowadays," was all he said.

They were aware there had been a change to his appearance since their last meeting. His left eye was badly bruised, not totally shut, but his vision was no doubt restricted due to the swelling. There was a deep graze across his left cheek as well as bruising around his neck, which he had tried to hide by wearing a shirt with a large collar. His left hand was bandaged around the wrist and across the thumb, it looked like a strain. He was not surprised that his guests were standing in the hallway staring at his injuries waiting for an explanation, which he quickly gave.

"I borrowed a pedal bike; my car was being serviced. I hadn't ridden one in years and won't be doing it again. Come out onto the patio, I've some beers if you want one."

Susan, having refused any refreshment, got straight to the point as they sat down.

"Why did you and Alan move a dead Frenchman from the airfield back to Alan's house. Then tell the world it was Alan on the floor?"

Martin admired Susan's brevity, Ian not so much. He took a long draft from his beer, paused a moment, then glanced at Martin and Susan with his wonky eye before letting out a deep breath.

"So, you found out. I guessed someone would in the end. This isn't going to be easy, but I'll be honest with you, it was a total farce that I got roped into." Again, he stopped his explanation, to twist off the cap of another bottle, sucked and cleared the exuding froth, then began his story.

He slowly explained that it had begun when one of the pilots was hanging around, wanting an overnight stay. He was ringing surrounding hotels for vacancies, which sometimes happened with international pilots. This one decided to drop dead. Ian admitted that he was all for calling the authorities, the right thing to do. But Alan stopped him, he said he had another plan, a plan which surprised Ian.

"He wanted us to take the body back to his house, then wanted me to call the ambulance saying it was him. I was gobsmacked, I can tell you. Of course, I asked him why he would want to appear dead. Well, there had to be a good reason, didn't there? But he was clear as a bell he wasn't going to share the motive with me, me being his best friend an' all, I was surprised."

Ian took another swig from the bottle before he admitted, "Best friends help one another and when Alan told me I had to trust him, well I couldn't refuse, could I?"

"Let's get this straight," Susan said, "as a favour to a mate, you moved a dead body, and then told a pack of lies to the powers that be without knowing why? Are you mad, or what?" Susan's bluntness was not lost on Ian.

"He offered me a thousand pounds to do it. Well, I thought he must have had a good reason to disappear. Of course, I helped him.

"We lifted the body into the back of my car, I took it to Alan's and we put it on the floor of the workshop. Alan had followed me back in his car. We had a few large whiskeys to calm our nerves. Just glad that no one saw us carry the body into the house. Alan drove back to the airport in my car, he said his own car needed to be parked outside his house to make it all look legit. I called the ambulance. Well, the rest you know."

"What if Alan's wife had had a look at the body. She'd have seen at once it was not her husband?" Martin asked, surprising himself that he had thought that one through.

"Alan reckoned not. He'd already called home to make sure she wasn't there, but she was obviously spending the night with a friend as she had told him that was her plan. She had always said she never wanted to see him dead. I did it partly 'cause Alan was a mate, who clearly wanted to disappear. The money helped. It seemed to be so easy. That was until the body fell out of the coffin. I ask you, how often does that happen? Now, I'm the one left holding the baby, so to speak. Alan has disappeared, just like he wanted."

"Is that all and is it the truth?" Martin asked.

"Honest, that's it. I've not heard from him from that day till this. Not a peep. He walked out the door and was gone, leaving me with a dead body. Now everyone is going to know that it was not Alan on the floor and I'm the one who's going to carry the can. And before you ask, I haven't seen a penny of the thousand pounds he promised."

"Where's your car now?" Susan asked, knowing that Ian needed it if he was going to continue his Uber taxi career.

"Outside, why?" Ian looked puzzled by the question; he had missed the significance of it.

"If Alan took it back to the airport for some reason. Then he might have thought it risky to drive it back here when he was meant to be on the floor dead."

"I picked it up from the shopping centre car park. That's where he said he'd be leaving it."

"He didn't say why he wanted to go back to the airport?"

"No, and I didn't think to ask. To be truthful, I was afraid."

Susan and Martin looked at each other, Ian being truthful, that would be a first. Did they believe everything he had said, maybe some of it, but they could not be certain it was all the truth. It was, however, the first out-loud admission by anyone that the body carted away by the undertakers was not Alan. At least Barry, and his reputation, were now in the clear and he could breathe a sigh of relief.

"Why would he want to fake his own death?" Susan asked once more, wondering what sort of excuse Ian might try to speculate.

"He did wonder if his old lady had a thing going with her boss. Maybe on the spur of the moment he decided to leave her and everything behind, I don't know."

"Or run off with his barmaid friend?"

"Doubt it, she was only a bit of a fling. That's all he did, a fling here and there, nothing serious. I'm being honest, I have no idea where Alan is or why he wanted to disappear."

"And you never thought to ask?"

"No. I know it seems stupid not to, but you got to think about how scared I was. Moving a dead body, well, it's just not right."

Martin, recalling their last visit, remembered a question that he and Susan had discussed. Why was it down to Alan to find a replacement for his injured colleague? If Ian was in the mood to confess, then now might be a good time to ask.

"Why did Alan need to find a temporary member of staff? Shouldn't the airport bosses have done that?"

Ian bowed down holding his head in his hands, he looked drained and tired. A liar who had been caught, and now another question he looked as if he was not happy about answering.

"I dunno. Alan said he'd pay me cash in hand for three weeks on nights. He needed someone he could trust. Extra bit of dosh and I could still do a bit of cabbing during the day. I'd be a fool not to."

"Did he pay you?"

"Yeah, every day, cash in the hand. It's just the grand he owes me."

"Where did he die?" Susan asked. "The French pilot, where was he when he dropped dead?"

Ian opened another bottle, while he thought back to that night.

"Alan found him. The plane was a late arrival, it was already dark when it landed, which surprised me. Alan told me that that sort of thing happens from time to time. He left me in the portacabin making a brew while he went over to speak to the pilot.

"Twenty minutes later he comes back, tells me the bloke has died. He made a couple of phone calls while I had a look at the bloke. Dead as a doornail beside his plane. The rest you now know."

"But you said that the pilot was hanging around, searching for a hotel?" Susan questioned.

"I just assumed. Alan had told me when we heard the plane landing that that was what happened from time to time."

They left with more information than when they arrived. They also had more questions that still needed answers.

As they left Ian to lock up his door firmly, Martin realised it would leave the afternoon free for him to grapple with IKEA instructions. But he was cunning or so he thought.

"Susan, let's have a nice lunch today, a bit of special time for you and me. A break from all this nonsense."

Susan leaned across towards the driver's seat where Martin had offered the invitation, first hugged him, then kissed him on the lips.

"That'll be great. Let's pop home first; I need to change."

***

Susan looked across the chipped red Formica-top table scowling at Martin. At that moment she wanted to stamp her feet and walk out or simply kill him. Instead, she told him, "You do know I hate you."

"Why, I'm being economic? I thought you'd be pleased."

"Thinking you were taking me somewhere fashionable for lunch, I put on my best jeans, a very fancy top, then spent a good deal of time on my make-up. I even put on that special gold bracelet, the one you bought for me on our honeymoon."

"And Nelly's Café is not fashionable enough for you?"

She leaned forward and whispered, "It's a transport café, a greasy spoon, a builder's restaurant."

"Maybe, but you must admit, it's cheap!" Martin smiled. It had not been easy finding a suitable eatery for a lunch that would give him change out of ten pounds. Thankfully, with the help of Google maps, he had found the perfect location.

Nelly's Café was located just a few miles from their house in Highfield. Apart from having plenty of good reviews, the café was a TV star. Well, more of a suitable location for the occasional drama as indicated by the memorabilia on the walls. The dominant colour was red. Red upholstered chairs with chrome frames. The counter was red with wood trimmings, even the trays were red. The floor was a very smart dark wood, not real wood, just patterned laminated boards.

Over the counter was written: 'Welcome to Nelly's', alongside which was an odd expression that Martin tried to make sense of, 'What if the 'Hokey Cokey IS what it is all about?', Martin had heard of the dance, just wasn't sure exactly what it was getting at. He dismissed his worries as the waitress, yes, dressed in red, served their food.

As she ate her Spanish omelette with chips, Susan felt the eyes of the other customers giving her a second look. She had dressed for a restaurant that had earned at least two Michelin stars, and here she was in a café with five hygiene stars, it could have been worse.

The two of them ate in taut silence, which Martin thought mildly comical as he ate egg, beans and chips. In the back of his mind, he planned to make it up to her tonight, after their visit to see Artemis. He had thought of a smart restaurant that he knew she would love.

Not that Susan was worried about what people were saying or thinking about her, she was not the type to care. It was more that Martin had thrown her words back in her face. She felt she had lost the argument over his excessive spending.

However, she did have a habit of seeing things work out in her favour in the end. Today that conclusion came with the sound of a familiar voice booming across the clamour of the café.

"Suzie baby, you're slumming it today. No rich men to ponce off?"

Only one person ever called her 'Suzie baby', that was the tall man walking towards her with a beaming smile, accentuated by the bright red lipstick he had applied. His ankle-length, floral skirt looked summery and fresh. She also noticed that Colin had tied his blonde hair in a French bun, although she suspected it might be a hair piece of some sort. Without waiting for an invite, he flopped down beside her, gave her a warm friendly hug, then turned to Martin.

"Is she leading you into the dark side of life? No tablecloths here, are there? Cotton or even paper ones. But they do a good Chai Latte."

"We're on a case," Susan admitted, not wanting to reveal the real reason they were in a greasy spoon cafe. Martin had other ideas.

"We are currently on an investigation, but we're also here because my wife wants to cut back on our expenditure."

Colin turned to Susan with a surprised look. "You, cutting back! Christ what next, giving up alcohol? Suzie baby, he's got loads in the bank, at least redistribute half of it. Money is to be enjoyed; you can't take it with you. What is it my old mum used to say, 'shrouds have no pockets', and she was right. And in return for such solid advice, I'll let you buy me lunch, which I'll eat while you tell me all about your current investigation."

The body falling out of the coffin brought tears of laughter to Colin's eyes, slightly smearing his dark blue mascara. The wife possibly having an affair with her boss, was greeted with a sigh of resignation, and the comment aimed at Susan, that falling for the boss was something she knew all about.

The report that Ian Cook was happy to lie about the identity of the dead body, only proved that some people would do anything for money. It also, Colin mentioned, showed how foolish some people are. "His mate had told him he planned to disappear off the face of the earth. Ian should have at the very least asked for the cash up front.

Serves him right." Colin had no sympathy for such stupidity.

The overall story of something being brought into the country by air, passed on and Alan receiving cash via the Asian man in the restaurant, that intrigued him. His many years as a police detective constable told him there was a whole sub-story yet to be uncovered, he needed more information.

"We know Alan is alive somewhere," Colin confirmed, "but the driver in the Tesco car park was not him, but the wife's boss or lover, possibly both. If the boss was in the car alone when he had the scrape, then the wife was in the store. Did you check the CCTV at the store entrance, see her go in and come out again?"

"I told you we should have done that," Susan exclaimed, pointing a finger at Martin.

"I said it was a waste of time, as she told us what she did," Martin countered. Only to hear Colin say,

"Martin, sweetheart, let's not be naïve here. She told you she was collecting supplies for refreshments in the office. From what you've told me, that Tesco seems a long way from where they work just to collect some digestive biscuits. It would be worth seeing what she did buy."

Susan recalled the odd visitor to the body in the Chapel of Rest which mystified Colin. Why had someone wanted a set of keys, and why were they in the brown suit in the first place?

Knowing human nature, Colin guessed that Alan would have a long-term lover somewhere. He would not disappear without a staging post or a safe place to prepare and finalise his plans to become someone else.

"But I still can't think why, on the spur of the moment, Alan decided that he wanted to vanish into thin air. It makes no sense. He left behind the house of which he would have owned half in the event of a separation. There must have been a more pressing reason for him to want to evaporate in a puff of smoke."

Colin had cleaned his plate and now drained the last of his Chai Latte. "Right, I'll leave you lovebirds to your romantic lunch. I'm off to Tesco to poke around and get some shopping. I'll be in touch."

With that he kissed Susan, stood up, ruffled Martin's hair, smiled and said, "Thanks for lunch, my treat next time. By the way, it might be worth your while going back to see Bill Latham at the airport, we have a dead flyer, but what's happened to his aeroplane?"

As Colin brushed down his skirt with his hands, his face portrayed a look of indecision. He hesitated for a moment then retook his seat. Leaned forward towards Martin.

"There's something I have been meaning to ask you." His tone was grave. When I was chauffeuring your mother around Grantham, we talked about the film The African Queen. Your mother was adamant that it was Dirk Bogarde in it. I know it was Humphrey Bogart. But we all make mistakes. There were a couple of other moments that weekend when I thought she was not quite herself. I was just a little worried and wanted to tell you. You know she's not getting any younger."

"Thanks Colin, it's nice of you to worry about my mother. Overall she is a tough old bean. But sometimes her mind does seem to wander off a bit. I don't think it's any more than just the fog of old age clouding her thinking."

"You don't know do you?" Susan asked Colin.

"Know what?"

"There is no need to go into details." Martin interrupted his wife.

"I think there is Martin, I'm defending your mother against you two writing her off as a doddery old lady."

"It doesn't matter, just ignore my wife." Martin tried to bring the direction of the conversation away from his mother. He knew he had failed when he heard Colin speak, leaning now towards Susan.

"Suzie baby you have intrigued me, tell all."

"Well." She began to explain with a broad grin. "Martin's mother in her younger years had a massive crush on Dirk Bogarde. Besotted with the film star she often refers to anyone with a similar name as being her heartthrob, Dirk. And not only that..."

"I bet Colin doesn't want to hear."

"I bet I do if you don't. Suzie baby pray continue."

"She wanted to call her only son, Dirk. But thankfully Mr Hayden put his foot down and insisted that his son was going to be called Martin. Although by way of a compromise my husband's full name is Martin Dirk Jules Hayden."

"Well I never, the things you learn across a Formica table are truly astounding."

"My middle names I do try to forget as best I can. Even Susan would never have found out had I not needed to produce my birth certificate for our wedding. Isn't that right Susan Florence Harriet Esmeralda Morris?"

"Oh God Suzie baby, tell me that's not true, honestly, Esmeralda! I think I'd best leave before you lovers have a tiff. I'll give you a bell later, oh sorry Suzie baby!" Colin walked out of the café laughing.

***

That evening, Potts Airfield still had its broken gates, worn-out sign, and a lone protester whom they waved to as they drove in. It looked no different from their last visit. The only thing that had changed were the workers who greeted them. Bill Latham and his mate were not working tonight.

The two men at the door looked very nervous to see two strangers in front of them. They did not display the same confidence that Bill had.

"How can we help you?"

"Bill not on tonight?" Susan asked, realising one of them, the one with the bright ginger hair had bad breath. She felt a little sorry for him.

"It's his night off, three on, three off, that's what we do here. Can we help you?"

"Maybe you can. We wanted to know a little more about Alan Hall and we're looking for a plane that might have lost its owner," Susan stated, noticing that the enquiry was confusing them. They invited their unexpected guests in, giving them more time to respond.

The four settled inside the portacabin, which had not changed noticeably since the Hayden's last visit. Ginger hair and the other man still looked concerned as to just what their visitors wanted from them.

"We did want to speak to Bill Latham, but you might well be able to help." Susan stood beside one of the lockers with a calendar of women in swimsuits which was two years out of date. Even further out of date if you took into account political correctness. "First off, you clearly know that Alan has died."

They nodded. Who hadn't heard that Alan was dead, then not dead, and now just maybe dead.

"What about the French pilot?"

This question produced a deeper look of mystery in them. They looked at each other, telepathically asking, should they know about a French pilot? Was it a trick question?

Susan looked around the squalid surroundings and noticed something she had not seen on her previous visit. She didn't bother waiting for an answer to her question which had stumped them.

She continued, "When Bill had his bike accident, would I be right in thinking Alan enlisted the help of his best friend for no better reason than he could trust him to keep your working practice a secret?"

"What secret?" The other worker, who wore a Newcastle hat, asked. There was a tremble in his voice. It was in fact the same question that Martin wanted to ask his wife: 'What secret are you talking about? Is there a secret?'

"That rota," Susan pointed to an A5 sized sheet of paper that was firmly attached to a shabby pinboard, "your shift patterns." She walked over, appearing to study the names and times before smiling at the sheet and speaking without looking at her audience.

"Today, Graham and George start at five pm. No doubt to carry out a hand over from the management here making sure you know what tasks are required. Then ten pm, Bill and Alan turn up to take over, until according to this, six am tomorrow morning. Oh look, it says the two of you get off work at midnight."

She turned to her audience, noting that the two employees had realised they had been caught out and Martin still looked totally confused.

Hence, she continued for the sake of her husband, who needed a simple explanation of such mundane things as shift patterns.

"As you said, that's the pattern until the day after tomorrow when it's Bill and Alan's turn to start at five. Would I be right in assuming that the late shift never turns up, the early shift covers for them. All the work is done by midnight and everyone is happy. Three days of work and three days off, with pay, not bad."

"That's rubbish," Ginger hair said.

"We were here on that day," she pointed to the night they had last visited the airport. "Alan and Bill were on early, but you were nowhere to be seen when we were here talking to Bill and his mate. Shouldn't they update this rota?"

"We do have an arrangement with the other shift workers and all the work gets done, that's the only thing that worries the bosses here. That's about it," Ginger hair replied, sitting down and dunking a digestive into a large JD Sports mega mug of tea. "When Bill came off his bike, there was no way he could get here, his knee was pretty banged up. So, we quickly had a pow-wow about the situation, we needed to work out the best way of keeping our little arrangement away from the bosses.

"The risk was that if Bill went on sick leave, then the bosses might send in a temporary worker. We could have possibly changed things around; you know to spread the workload between the three of us. But I have another job on my nights off. Well, I say off, I mean when I'm not here.

"In the end, Alan suggested that Bill just stays away until he's better, not claim sick leave. He had a mate who would help, and he would pay him in cash until Bill could come back."

"Lucky for us," Newcastle Hat took up the saga, "when Alan died, Bill was just about fit enough to come back, and he had a trusted friend who could stand in for Alan."

"Did Bill pay his friend's wages as well?" Susan asked Newcastle Hat wondering where all the money was coming from.

"Yeah, real lucky. But now, everyone knows that Alan has died, even the bosses, so they are planning to advertise. It looks like from next week we might all need to come in."

"Only for a while, I hope. I need to take annual leave from my other job," Ginger complained as he finished his third dunked digestive.

"Well thanks," Martin began to wrap up the conversation, he was getting hungry and wanted to get back home. Susan though, still had another question.

"What about the plane that came after dark the night Alan died?"

The two workers looked at each other, thinking the woman was having a funny turn.

It was Newcastle Hat who answered with a newfound confidence, "Impossible, the runway has no lights. We never get planes here at night. As soon as dusk falls, all aerial movements are off."

"We have it on good authority that the body previously known as Alan, belongs to a dead French pilot, who landed here after dark the night Alan was supposed to have died. Where would that plane be now?"

Ginger laughed as he opened a new packet of digestives, all these questions were making him hungry.

"Trust me, if you wanted to land a plane here at night, then it would be a bit like driving around the M25 blindfolded. If, and only if, you did manage it, then you could park your plane wherever you liked. The management here have no idea what's going on, be it day or night, as our amended shift pattern proves."

"Okay, what about this. How well did you know Alan, given that you're supposed to work together?" Susan asked not sure what she was expecting by way of an answer.

Newcastle Hat said he had worked with Alan a few times. It was the nature of their arrangement that when someone wanted some time off which did not fit in with the rota, they would help each other out.

He recalled that earlier in the year, when Bill Latham went on a two-week jaunt around Scotland on his bike, he stood in and worked with Alan for that time. He concluded that Alan was a top-notch bloke, always smiling and a laugh as well. When confronted with the question about any clandestine romances, Newcastle Hat just frowned, thought for a moment or two then concluded, 'never in a million years', Alan was just too nice to do such a thing. Happy to give an example he pointed out that one night Alan told him he could go home, take the night off, well, that was decent of him. He was considerate about my having to work more consecutive days than normal, he said.

"But he changed," Ginger was putting in his view. "Ever since he had his bike nicked, he's been as grumpy as hell every time I spoke to him."

"Explain," Martin spoke, sounding a little too much like one of his gowned tutors at school.

"Well, he said he was filling up his bike, went in to pay, and someone had his bike away. Ever since then he's been as jumpy as hell. Don't know why, he was insured, but he has been tetchy ever since."

"Now you mention it, you're right," Newcastle Hat agreed. "Last time I saw him, maybe a week or so before he died or whatever he has done, really snapped at me when I asked if he was going on holiday anytime soon."

"I'd be annoyed if it was my collector's bike that was stolen," Susan agreed.

"Not his posh bike," Newcastle Hat pointed out, "the Triumph only came out at weekends. It was his Yamaha that he comes to work on that was nicked."

"And him outside, mister one man demo," Susan asked her last question, as she had seen that Martin was already holding onto the door handle in anticipation of their departure. "Aren't you worried he might spill the beans?"

Ginger, having finished his drink, stood up respectfully, sensing the guests were about to leave. "Who old man Archie Nihill? He only cares about his aliens."

Susan and Martin recognised the name in an instant.

***

Not used to having people approach him, Archie Nihill struggled up from his foldable stool. He was wearing the same heavy coat and black scarf they had seen him wearing the last time they passed this one-man protest. In his late seventies, sitting for hours on end in the cold did not do him a lot of good, it just made him feel worthwhile that he had a crusade. He was not sitting around watching TV, waiting for death, he was sitting around hopefully making a difference.

These two young people seemed interested in his campaign, more so than the few others that walked past him did. The airfield management had taken a dislike to him from the moment he and some other residents succeeded in putting a stop to the plans to enlarge the airfield. He preferred the evening shift with fewer people to try and move him on and the men in the portacabin gave him hot drinks and free sandwiches.

Now he was standing up, Martin was surprised at how tall Archie was. Even with a slightly arched back, he looked to be about six foot three.

"You were here the other night," Archie stated, recalling the couple who had waved amiably to him as they drove away.

"We were indeed." Susan, acting like his granddaughter, adjusted his scarf to ensure it was snug fitting. "If you're going to protest, make sure you keep warm."

"You sound like my daughter, always fussing over me."

"Wouldn't it be better if you did this during the day."

"Bit of a blip on the landscape for the powers that be. Hate to be reminded that people power stopped their hideous expansion plans."

"But if you have succeeded in stopping the airfield getting bigger, why are you still here?" It was an obvious question that Susan asked. She ignored the alien references on the placards and what the staff had told her.

However, he pointed down at the signs wagging his finger. "There is alien activity here that people need to be aware of. I've tried telling the control tower, but they just think I'm a mad old man who wants to see the airfield gone. That's not the case.

"Some nights I see lights in the sky circling the airport when there should be nothing here. You can also hear them. I think that the real reason they wanted a concrete runway here was so they could land bigger spacecraft.

"But we stopped that plan in its tracks. So now they continue their nocturnal flights, bringing in supplies and weapons. Potts Field will be a forward base for the aliens, of that I can assure you."

Archie then began a long homily about the way beings from Teegarden's star system were using Potts Field to store supplies as well as explore the surrounding countryside. He said they circled the landing strip three times before turning out their lights and then landing. He had also seen a light on the airfield, no doubt to guide in the spacecraft. He had only heard a few taking off but put forward his theory that in one of the aircraft hangars was an instantaneous transporter machine, which could send the empty freight spaceship back to Teegarden. Susan and Martin listened tolerantly.

The only reason they wanted to talk to the old man was that his name was in the visitor's book at Gladstone Funeral Directors, the visitor who appeared to have paid their respects to Alan. The more he spoke, the less likely they thought he would do such a thing. He was noticeably tall, which Pete did not mention. The limp that was cited did not appear as Archie walked along the fence, pointing out the direction of the spaceships as they made their approach. It was clear his name had been used; it was not him at the funeral parlour. Martin hoped that even though Archie was eccentric, he might be methodical.

Fortuitously he was, and he could provide them with proof from the log that he kept of all the alien activity that took place the night the French pilot died.

"Here we are." He was proud of his A4 red and black book with its neat entries in his spidery writing. He pointed to the date Martin had asked for and recited the entry.

"Lights seen in the sky: 21.45. Heard the landing five minutes later. Nothing else after that. They either took off using their transportation machine or I fell asleep."

Susan smiled warmly at the old man; it was good to know that national security was in such safe hands.

Chapter 15

His original plan envisaged wearing a different pair of trainers for every day of the year. To Artemis, who since childhood had a passion for trainers, this made perfect sense. They were after all high-quality foot apparel which told observers about you as a person, as well as making you feel good. Nike Air Jordans were his shoe of choice, other brands he might buy on a whim, or because he thought they suited him. But inevitably he would return to Nike Air Jordans or sometimes another shoe from the Nike range.

After his divorce, Artemis bought this house with the sole objective of dedicating one room to his fixation for trainers and the quest for having one pair for each day of the year. He moved in with one hundred and five boxed pairs, which he carefully and methodically stacked against a wall in the room he designated as his Temple of Trainers. The same room that neighbours along the street would have called the spare bedroom.

The Temple was an ideal place to fix on one of its walls a map of the United Kingdom County boundaries. It was big, the largest map he could find, which he mounted on a large sheet of cork. It was a shade under seven feet tall, which meant the Isles of Scilly were down on the skirting board, John o'Groats was almost touching the ceiling. The Orkneys and Shetlands were on a separate map to the right of the main map.

Although the county boundaries were clearly shown, Artemis also wanted to mark out the parliamentary constituencies across the country. This he did over several weeks. The next stage was to pin small flags on the map, indicating the political party which had won that district. He would then cross reference the results to his Excel spreadsheet which he regularly updated following by-elections. Post general elections he took a week's annual leave to ensure the Excel sheet and the map were accurate.

Almost two years had passed since he had moved into the house and the map was just about complete, save for two by-elections which took place about four weeks earlier. His collection of trainers had grown, he now had one hundred and fifty-three boxed trainers. Nike Air Jordans were to the left of the pile in numerical order. Those to the right were various other brands, ordered by colour. It was at this point he faced a quandary.

The wall where he was building his collection of trainers was seven feet high and just about ten feet wide. It was the biggest wall area in the room. Yet a quick calculation brought home the fact he was not going to get more than two hundred and forty boxes against this wall. Just under two thirds of his target.

The next wall was dominated by a window, so it had little useable space. The following side was even smaller, plus there was a door reducing the area available still further. The next biggest wall was the location for the UK constituency map. On either side of the map, avoiding the Orkney and Shetlands appendix, were shelves to accommodate tomes of electoral reference books.

It was a conundrum which he felt he could not overcome without moving into another room, which he did not want to do. This was his room. This was his shelter from the world. Also, all the others were in various stages of redecoration. It looked highly likely that he would not achieve his goal of wearing a different trainer each day.

The doorbell, the European Union anthem, Ode to Joy, echoed around the house. His expected visitors had arrived. He wondered if Martin and Susan had uncovered anything interesting. He also hoped they would be quick, so with that in mind, he invited them into the living room omitting to offer any refreshment.

As Susan began to summarise the last couple of days, she wondered just why Artemis found it so comfortable to sit in a loose-fitting t-shirt depicting a past tour of a band called Vulcano, whom she had never heard of. If that was not bad enough, he wore a pair of baggy loose-fitting shorts with a colourful design which looked almost floral in an abstract way. Even indoors he was wearing trainers, which she recognised as Air Jordans, it was the black socks he was also wearing that made them look less cool.

"What era are Vulcano from? I've never heard of them," Susan questioned.

"Well, you have no idea the excitement and sheer pleasure you're missing out on. Vulcano are a Dutch band known for their big hits such as 'Shut up and Boogie', or the evergreen 'Secret Groin'. Regrettably they broke up in 1986, I have a music cassette of theirs which I will dig out for you. But first an update I feel will be in order."

Artemis listened without comment as Susan told him that it was highly likely that the dead body, was that of a French pilot who had died of a heart attack at Potts Field Airport. The reason that Alan wanted to pass the body off as himself, stemmed from the possibility that some commodity was being transited through the airport by the pilot with the cooperation of Alan and Bill. The Haydens agreed Ian was possibly an innocent party in that respect.

But there was a need for the body to be disposed of to avoid Alan and Bills' activities being discovered.

There was compelling evidence that money was changing hands between Alan and Max Phillips who used his companion, the Indian man, to contact Alan.

Martin admitted that they had no idea why Alan might want to disappear from the world by insisting the dead French man was buried under his name. It could, Martin pointed out, have something to do with the supposition that his wife, Christine, was possibly having an affair with her boss.

"Interesting," was all Artemis said as he linked his fingers together forming an arch.

"Plus, we know," Susan said, trying not to obviously stare at the t-shirt, "Alan and his work colleague, Bill, appeared to have plenty of cash to spend employing people they trusted to act as temporary workers at the airfield. What they were transporting we aren't sure, but drugs are a popular commodity these days if you want to make serious money."

"Could it be the Asian man is responsible for importing drugs, or do you think Mr Phillips is involved?" There was a hint of genuine concern in his voice which Susan found strange.

"I'd have money on the old man being the driving force and collecting all the profits. I would guess his man around the house is just that, his handyman."

"Well, that all sounds very plausible given what I have uncovered." Artemis smiled and took a sheet of paper from the small table beside him, referring to it when he next spoke. "As we expected, Alan has made no credit or debit card transactions since he, shall we now say, disappeared?

"His last card transaction was for three pounds fifty at Greggs bakers, not an extravagant lunch. His phone record, however, offered a little more information. As we know his last call was to the old man, Max Phillips. What I didn't grasp at the time was that if you make a call and it isn't answered, then it comes up in a different report." He waved the paper in his hand before continuing, "Alan, after calling Mr Phillips, called his home number, possibly checking that his wife had really gone away. That corresponds with the version Ian has given.

"I next had a peek at Max Phillip's mobile telephone record. That shows that straight after his 'wrong number' from Alan, he called a French mobile number. He spoke for three minutes, which fits in very well with your dead French pilot theory. The pieces of the jigsaw are now coming together."

"No other calls?" Susan asked. "Was that the last call he made?"

"No more that night."

Susan added that they believed the visitor to the Chapel of Rest was Bill Latham. He quite possibly still had a limp from his injury when he popped in, presumably to collect a set of keys that had been mistakenly hidden in the suit.

The purpose of the keys, she suggested with the gravitas of Sherlock Holmes, was the key to a mystery place where Alan had no doubt stashed the contraband from that night's delivery. Maybe Bill needed to get to it.

Artemis stood up, brushed off some imaginary fluff from his t-shirt and smiled broadly.

"It has become increasingly clear that Mr Max Phillips is at the centre of a group who are importing something, which they don't want any authority to look at. I support you Susan, drugs do seem to be the most likely cargo.

"Hence, we also now know that Alan is alive somewhere. I think together we have completed our task. I can't thank you enough for your help. Please charge me for the whole of the day. Your contribution has been more than valuable."

Martin stood up with a smug look. He was dwarfed by Artemis as he walked over, shook his hand, thanked him, and wished him well for the future. All the while Susan remained firmly seated wearing a frown reflecting her bewilderment.

She had taken part in a few cases since she had joined Hayden Investigations. She would be the first to admit that she wasn't highly trained or had any form of detecting qualification. But she knew when a case was at the end, when it had reached a conclusion and as far as she could see, this case was nowhere near any sort of conclusion. They had strong theories, a raft of evidence and a lot of circumstantial proof. But they hadn't ended this investigation and she was going to make that point.

"Hold on, what are you two going on about. We haven't finished, we have made progress but are far from finished."

Artemis looked down at her, she appeared small in his eyes.

"You've done enough. I will pass on all that we've learned to the police, they will continue to investigate. I would imagine, in the fullness of time, Max and his man, Bill and possibly Ian will be arrested. Perhaps they will also be able to, given their resources, trace Alan wherever he's hiding and charge him. I think we can all agree drug smuggling is the most likely crime here and the police are very good at solving crimes."

"No, no, no! When we took on this case, you said that your company wouldn't pursue it. You wanted to find the husband to avert the wife having to give up her house through no fault of her own."

"Quite so Susan. However, we now know that Alan isn't dead. It's very likely that he's a man on the run, maybe with a large consignment of stolen drugs. As you mentioned earlier, you suspect Ian's injuries were administered by Max Phillips to try and ascertain the whereabouts of Alan. He would only have done that if Alan had something valuable, perhaps as we imagine, a load of precious drugs.

"Therefore, Alan's on the run from a criminal gang which might not end well. If the police catch him first, then he'll be spending many years in prison. That won't help the wife in the least, with or without a lover.

"Your initial brief was to pressure the wife to see if she might be in cahoots with her husband to fake his death and defraud my insurance company. Clearly that isn't the case. Also, by uncovering his deception, we clear the funeral directors of any administration error. It's now a matter for the police."

If Artemis thought the calm, firm explanation of his viewpoint would have any effect on Susan, he was mistaken. She slapped her hands against the arms of the chair.

"We can't just stop and walk away, that isn't how Hayden Investigations operates."

"Isn't it?" Martin asked not sure which side he should align himself to. The most obvious was Artemis, who was after all standing them down from any further work. There again, he was married to Susan, and he would have to at some time capitulate, if not today, one day soon. He still had Verona very much in his mind.

"No Martin, it isn't. When the Haydens investigate a case, we see it through to the end. Wherever the clues lead us, we go, until it's concluded."

"But you must see the point Artemis is making. Max Phillips is no doubt a big-time drug dealer, importing from abroad. We're not dealing with some pensioner selling a little bit of weed, like the case in Grantham. This is serious and dangerous stuff which we should pass onto the police."

Susan remained seated, thinking how to counter their arguments. Maybe it would be dangerous, but she had learnt that nothing comes easy and walking away was not something you should do just because the consequences might be dire. She had also learnt that if you're in a corner with the wolves snapping at you, you need to give them a distraction and she had one.

"What about the bike?" she asked.

"Bike, what are you talking about?"

"Alan having a bike stolen a few weeks ago, something you hadn't mentioned before. Did he claim on the insurance?"

"Oh that. I doubt if it has anything to do with what we're currently dealing with. He'd left his bike to go and pay for petrol when an unknown person stole it. A simple theft, I didn't think it important."

"Didn't think it important! That's very naive of you," Susan responded, not even sure herself of the significance of the theft. But she was after all trying to deflect Artemis from closing the case. "His mood changed after that theft. It must be significant." Well, she hoped it was, although she was not convinced herself.

"Susan, your enthusiasm is truly commendable, but it's now time to hand everything over to the police."

She was not going to accept that, not in a million years.

Chapter 16

Just as before, the door opened and a tall Asian man with a missing thumb looked down at her. He wore the same look of distrust as when he had previously seen her standing in front of him.

Susan swallowed dramatically. She could never work out just why such an action might calm your nerves, but for her it worked.

"I need to see Mr Phillips; I have news that I know he'll want to hear."

If she was being honest with herself, Mr Phillips might not want to know that Alan Hall was, according to Ian, still alive. Alive somewhere, probably with a stash of drugs, worth a small fortune that belonged to him.

Susan had been annoyed, more like incensed, that her husband and Artemis wanted to stop the investigation and hand everything over to the police. She wasn't surprised that Martin was happy to pass on everything to someone else. All he had been focused on during the last few days was their trip to Verona. Of course, she wanted to go, who wouldn't? Three weeks in Italy, good food and good wine, what was there not to like?

She was surprised that Artemis, being a professional, was happy to step away. Susan was of the opinion, if you start something you should see it through to the end.

Last night, neither Martin nor Susan had spoken much to each other, there was an atmosphere in the house. Then Martin had left this morning to get himself fitted with new clothes for Verona. As soon as he had gone, Susan grabbed her car keys and made her way to the house of Max Phillips. She was going to have it out with him. Tell him all she knew; she was convinced that between the two of them they could work out where Alan might be.

She had been full of bravado as she parked. That bravado receded as she looked up into the eyes of the Asian man with the missing thumb and saw a very serious look, recalling that this sweet-looking man could well have been the cause of Ian's 'bike injuries'.

"You had better come in then."

The door was opened and held back for her, unlike last time. She was not sure if that was a good thing or a bad thing. Just as any efficient butler would, the Asian man showed Susan into the room where Max Phillips was again at his desk reading the Racing Post.

"This young lady believes that she has some news that you will find interesting." Without waiting for a reply, he turned to walk out.

Before he closed the door Max called after him, "I'll need the car in five minutes."

Max closed the racing paper and turned his attention to Susan.

"I hope this will be quick. I'm about to leave for Lingfield and watch my horses hopefully win. So, what's your news young lady?"

Her bravado had receded even further as she looked at Max who was still wearing his stripy blazer and matching fedora. He was plump and intimidating.

"You say your horses, are we talking ones that you've backed or yours as in owning them?"

"I own two horses, both of which, by a quirk of fate are running today, not in the same race, but at the same racecourse. Your news?"

"Which track are they using today, the all-weather?" Just why Susan had decided to veer the conversation towards horse-racing when she had planned to confront him with being a drug dealer, was a lot to do with her now questioning why she was here in the first place. It had seemed a good idea back in the safety of her own home, but now, she wanted to put off the inevitable confrontation.

"All-weather, a formula that suits my horses, they like the consistent surface. One hates the soft and the other hates the good going, they can be very fussy, almost like prima donnas. Now do you have some news for me?"

"Alan Hall is still alive," she blurted out.

Max carefully folded the Racing Post into a size smaller than A5, quite a feat Susan thought, then pushed it into his blazer side pocket. "Why would that fact be of any interest to me?"

She swallowed, gripped the arms of the chair a little too tightly and said, "He has something of yours that you want back. I want to find him as much as you do, maybe together we can. Then you get your merchandise back and his wife gets him back."

There she had said it, maybe poorly phrased, but she had said it. She wanted to work in co-operation with a drug dealer to get a man back to his wife. Bring Alan back from the dead, even if he ended up in prison.

Max stood up, picked up his phone from the desk and placed it carefully inside his blazer.

"Do you follow horse racing young lady? Not everyone knows that there's an all-weather track at Lingfield."

"I wouldn't say I'm a gambler. My father liked the gee-gees and had a regular flutter. I just overheard him and have followed the sport from a distance."

"Well, can I invite you to join me and see it up close? Then we can discuss Alan Hall in a comfortable atmosphere; the owners' bar is a very acceptable venue. Come, Archibald should be waiting for us in the car."

The back of the car, where Susan was now sitting alongside Max, was luxurious. The deep comfy leather seats made her feel relaxed as Archibald drove the Lexus smoothly along the busy roads.

Max spoke as he looked out of the window watching the suburban houses effortlessly pass by. "What do you think Alan could possibly have of mine?"

"Drugs," was all she said, bluntly and to the point. In the main because what she had said out loud seemed to concentrate her thoughts and bring into focus exactly where she was.

In the back of a car, obviously. Sitting next to a drug dealer. Not your run of the mill on the corner dealer, passing on a few pills and wraps, this man arranged for drugs to be flown in from France and delivered under cover of darkness to an insignificant airfield. He had a number of people around him, including Alan, to ensure everything went smoothly and secretly. Max was a big drug dealer. Of course, Artemis and Martin might have pointed that out, but sitting next to him, here and now, made it very real. Plus, a little bit scary, she admitted to herself.

Not only that, but she was also being driven to Lingfield, or so she was being told, she knew they were heading in the general direction of Lingfield. But the racecourse, she realised, was in the Surrey countryside, an area with small-wooded sections, lonely spots, unseen roads, ideal places to get rid of someone. In that moment she was very scared.

"Drugs," Max repeated. "Interesting. You're right, it would be in our joint benefit to find Mr Hall. Do you have any clues as to where we might locate him?"

That was the thing, Susan knew a lot, but not enough to even hazard a guess as to where Alan might have concealed himself or the drugs. Things got worse when Max pointed out that she had little to offer him by way of information. Then he asked if her husband knew anymore. She pointed out that Martin knew even less. Of course, he knew as much as she did, but unconsciously she was protecting him as best she could.

"Does your husband know you've come to see me?"

"Of course," she snapped back quickly to make it sound like the truth.

"But he doesn't know you're in the back of my car going to the races, because you had no idea you would be until I invited you."

If Max was playing mind games with Susan, he was winning. She began to work out a plan to escape. They might still be going in the direction of Lingfield, but until they drove into the car park, she was mapping out a strategy to get out of the car. She was regretting even thinking about speaking to Max let alone visiting him. She took out her phone, the screen was black. She pressed the power button – nothing. She chastised herself, her phone was dead, she had thought about charging it last night, but had not got around to it. Things had gone from bad to worse.

***

It had been a very good morning for Martin; the sort of day he enjoyed. A mid-morning appointment with his tailor – Norton's – for a fitting. That only took an hour as most of his measurements had remained static, save for half an inch on his waist, which his tailor put down to him now being married.

Next, he popped into a local wine bar to see an old friend. He had not seen 'Freddie the Frog' since the wedding and they had a lot to catch up on. Martin had known him since his school days. Like most of the boys there, he was known by a nickname. Frederick Van Houten, to use his correct name, had a habit of leaping from social event to social event to dine on free food, hence the reference to a frog.

The great thing about Freddie was his job as a professional socialite, something Martin always envied. What he did not have any intention of copying was Freddie's loud dress sense, which today consisted of a bright pink shirt, very light blue chinos and a yellow silk scarf. He had always thought his school friend should have been named Flamboyant Freddie.

"Do you remember Pinky?" Freddie asked, having cleared his cheese plate with the same gusto he applied to all his food.

"Pinky Pead, yes still catch-up with him once in a while. He was planning to come to the wedding, but something came up. Why do you ask?"

"Saw him the other day at Launceston Place, we had lunch. The place has gone downhill of late, but he was paying. Anyway, he asked about you and your detective agency. Asked if you were any good. I sang your praises. Mentioned the case about the old lady dying I helped you out with. He didn't elaborate; maybe he plans to go into competition with you."

"Well, we don't worry too much about any commercial rivals."

"I'm surprised you're even bothering to investigate, but that's wives for you," Freddie laughed loudly. If there was one thing he was not shy about, it was making a spectacle of himself.

Now one good meal and two bottles later, Martin was sitting in the back of an Uber returning home. He felt relaxed, peaceful, and looking forward to an evening with Susan. He had been a little off with her last night, well, why did she think it a good idea to continue the investigation. Artemis was right, it was now time for the police to take over. Tonight, he planned to indulge her and be the attentive husband he always hoped he would be.

Saying sorry without actually speaking the words, he planned to cook for her tonight. That would be a grand gesture, a sort of reconciliation, not that they had had an argument. Although he would never consider himself to be a good cook, or even an adequate one, he could knock up a mean meatball pasta, if there was one of those readymade sauces in the cupboard and a bag of furniture shop meatballs she had bought in the freezer. All he needed to do was to add a few herbs and chilli to the sauce and hey presto, a Michelin starred meal for two. He smiled to himself, thanked the driver and wandered into the house.

"Susan, I'm back," he called out. He listened for her reply as he took off his coat. Silence, again he called out, "Susan, where are you hiding? I've got a plan for tonight." The house remained soundless. He went from room to room, occasionally calling her name.

The house was empty. How stupid of him, as he looked out at the drive and saw her car was not there, how had he missed that? Well, no doubt she had gone shopping. Martin put on the kettle, made himself a coffee and settled down with The Telegraph.

He looked at his watch. It had been over an hour since he had arrived home. He sent a message, 'Home and I'm cooking tonight. What time do you want to eat?'

Ten minutes seemed like two hours. Martin was worried, she had not even read the message. He sent another, 'What are you up to?' Ten more minutes and still nothing. It was now after five o'clock, he was starting to feel concerned.

This was so unlike Susan. At times she could be irritating with her texting, Facebook posts and quick phone calls to say nothing much. But now he really wanted her to ring him. He thought about calling her friend Becky, maybe she would know. There again he did not want to seem to be the worried husband overreacting. He waited impatiently. It was quarter past six when he heard the sound of tyres driving across gravel. He glanced through the window, trying to conceal himself. It was Susan's car. He settled back down in the chair with his paper, wanting to present the image of a nonchalant husband. He spoke as she walked into the room, "Where have you been?" Which came out a little too gruff to be that of a relaxed husband.

Susan flopped down onto the sofa opposite Martin, kicked off her shoes and leaned back, she looked tired. "Horse racing. I bet you thought I was shopping," she smiled.

"Horse racing!" Martin repeated.

"Yes. And before you ask who I went with, just remember I'm back here safe and sound. Although to be honest I do think I might be close to the drink drive limit, but I'm safe."

Martin's first thought was Becky, Susan's friend, who when they met up on whatever pretext, they normally ended up in an establishment serving alcohol. Watching horse racing did not seem to be Becky's thing. Susan's dad, Martin knew enjoyed a little flutter on the horses now and then. It would not be beyond the bounds of possibility that she had gone with her father, although he would not have let her drive home after a drink. Darkly he wondered if it might be an ex-boyfriend. While he was sure Susan would not take up any offer from an ex, could he be mistaken?

"Alright, who did you go with?"

"Max Phillips. He owns two racehorses and he invited…"

"Max Phillips, the drug dealer. Why would he call you and invite you to a horse race?"

"He didn't call, I popped round to see him."

"Let me get this straight. We are talking about the Max Phillips whom we believe is importing large volumes of drugs into this country illegally. The same Max Phillips whom Artemis and I suggested should be brought to the attention of the police, given that any interaction with him, for example investigating his activities, might become a dangerous occupation. That Max Phillips?"

"Well, he's the only one we know. Yeah, nice chap and offered..."

"He's a bloody drug dealer, a criminal! What on earth were you doing in his company?"

"Language please Martin. There's no need for any profanities. As I said I'm safe and sound."

"But you popped round to see him! What were you going to ask him, 'can I borrow a cup of sugar?'"

"Don't be so stupid Martin, I told him that we wanted to find Alan Hall. I suggested that he might also like to talk to him because he might have something of his that he wants back. He was very upfront and honest about the whole thing. But sadly, he has little idea where Alan might be, so we kind of drew a blank, as I haven't the foggiest where he is either. But we've agreed to co-operate. Then he invited me to Lingfield racecourse, owners' bar, up close and personal with the jockeys and trainers. It was a great afternoon."

"But you're missing my point. He's a big criminal, the sort of person who we think beats up best friends to get information out of them. He is, in a word, dangerous and not a person I think you should hang out with."

"You can be so sweet and caring at times Martin. He was very attentive. For example, while we were in the owners' lounge, – loads of posh people there – he had a visitor. Well, one of the waiters told him that a person called Tony wanted to see him urgently. Politely he said no as he was with an important guest and didn't want to be disturbed.

"Turns out this Tony is his stepbrother, I told him family should always come first. But then he took me through his family history, mum and dad splitting up, the mum married again and had a couple of kids. One being this Tony. Looked me in the eye and said, 'you can't choose your family, but you can choose your friends.' A real gentleman."

"Who sells drugs and ignores his stepbrother." Martin added.

"But think about it for a moment, he doesn't have a criminal record, Artemis told us that. He's therefore very shrewd and no doubt keeps naughty things very much at arm's length. He wasn't going to kill me."

"Not yet. But in the end, it was a waste of time," Martin pointed out folding his newspaper, standing, and thinking it was time to start cooking and opening the wine.

"Not entirely," Susan beamed, and pulled a wad of notes from her pocket, waving them at Martin. "Two-thirty-five race, a little mare called Hacker des Places. Odds of twenty-five to one and who put a tenner on it? Yours truly. Two hundred and fifty smackers. I wouldn't call that a waste of time, would you?"

"No." Martin walked out of the room in a bit of a mope, aware that Susan was following him into the kitchen.

"Plus, things get better, it looks like you're cooking tonight. Oh, and I have an address."

Martin stopped in the hallway and turned towards her. What sort of address he wondered, but suspected whatever it was it was not going to be important. "Gamblers Anonymous. Criminals incorporated. Tell me."

"Alan Hall's mistress." She offered a sheet of paper to him, a scruffy sheet with a handwritten address.

"Max gave you that?"

"No, his bloke, Archibald. Although I never called him that all afternoon, stupid name anyway. I called him Archie, which he seemed to like. His real name is Ali, but Max can be a bit presumptuous at times.

"After the races they took me back to their place, that's where my car was parked. Max goes inside, a little miffed if I am honest, neither of his horses won or even placed. Archie makes sure I get to my car okay; it was parked down the road.

"He hands me this sheet of paper, saying, 'it's Alan's long-term mistress'. Alan wasn't there when Archie called on her. She said she didn't know where he was, but he didn't believe her. Thought it might help us. We now have a new line of inquiry."

Martin handed the scrap of paper back without even so much as a smile. He wasn't happy that she had, in his opinion, put herself in danger. She could be so single minded at times. It was a trait he liked, yet wished she only used it in certain circumstances. He walked into the kitchen, Susan still following him.

The kitchen was empty of builders as they had gone earlier in the day leaving behind a room that could be used, yet was a mess. The wall cupboards had been taken down, resulting in many oddly coloured squares on the wall. All the kitchen base units no longer had doors. Thankfully there was still a worktop where Martin had his beloved microwave plugged in. In one corner was a stack of toolboxes and dust sheets as well as a battered radio. He had to move a pair of steps to get to the freezer which was in the middle of the room, uncomfortably close to the table and chairs.

He was searching around for the ingredients to create the meal. Without looking at Susan he spoke, "Anything else you haven't told me?"

"Only a sort of confession from Max, or maybe it was an omission. I think confessions are things you do in church. Anyway, he told me there was nothing to connect him to Alan, whatever I said or accused him of."

"You accused him?"

"No, just said I knew he was dealing drugs. He smiled, then said, it would be impossible to prove in court that it was not a wrong number when Alan called him. He and Alan had never been companions. It was just a coincidence that his butler – yes, he called him a butler – went to the same restaurant as Alan. The two never spoke.

"Finally, he admits at the racecourse, I think he was a little under the influence of alcohol by this time, that he's just a middleman, low risk, high profit. He turns out to be a bit of an arrogant old man with an odd fashion sense."

Martin began stirring the sauce straight from the jar. He popped the meatballs into the microwave, then put the water on to boil for the pasta. Any attempted cooking had to be quick and easy for him; unlike this current investigation. "I suppose we will be going to see the mistress tomorrow?"

"You bet yer bottom dollar!"

Chapter 17

"I think I should have furnished the dining room before having the kitchen dismantled," Susan admitted as she finished her meatballs at the kitchen table. It was not the best place to eat. She had suggested that they had the meal on their laps in the living room while watching TV, which didn't impress Martin in the least. Reluctantly he sat at the table, which first had to be wiped clean of dust as did the chairs before they sat down.

Apart from the chaotic environment Martin regarded the meal a reasonable success. The pasta was okay, the meatballs, while not the best he had ever tasted, coming from a furniture store he had had low expectations of them anyway. The sauce was out of a jar, nothing to go wrong there. Finally, and most importantly the wine, a French Bordeaux that they were consuming together, it was softening the tension that he felt earlier. He was thankful that Susan was home and safe, chatting away like there was no tomorrow following her day at the races.

He recalled during a previous investigation, she had shown herself to be knowledgeable regarding horse racing, impressing a regular gambler. She must have made a comparable impression on Max, hence the spontaneous invitation to join him at Lingfield. The thing was, he knew that outside of those examples, she showed little interest in the sport. Never placed bets on horses, save for the times she was there socially, or maybe on one of the big annual races that the world and its mother gambled on.

"How come you know so much about horse racing? I know you've said in the past your dad had a flutter, but that doesn't require the level of knowledge you seem to possess."

"I just read and retained a lot of the knowledge."

"Liar," Martin was swift in his accusation. He could see the guilt in her eyes, and how uncomfortable she was as she shuffled in her chair and sipped on her drink.

"That's a bit cruel."

"Maybe, but I know you well enough to know when you aren't telling the whole story."

Susan topped up their glasses. She was preparing for a confession when interrupted by the doorbell.

Artemis stormed in when Martin answered the door. He sat down at the table without any formal invitation to join them, still dressed in shorts, plainer than he had worn before. His t-shirt was praising a band that had long since passed into the annals of music history. He came straight to the point; Martin had not even sat down.

"Susan, what in heaven's name were you doing this afternoon in the company of Max Phillips at a racecourse?"

"Were you at the races too?"

"That wasn't an answer, I'm asking the questions. Social or business?" Artemis persisted.

"I think," Martin was not going to let any man speak to his wife in such a way, "you should calm down, take a deep breath and think for a moment. The last time you spoke to Susan, she wasn't pleased about the idea of quitting the investigation. If you used some of that logic you are so proud of, then you might understand that she was there on business. Taking, I should point out, a considerable risk."

Artemis looked at him, then turned to Susan and back to Martin before finally returning his gaze to Susan.

"I believe I told you the matter was going to be passed onto the police, there was no need for you to continue. It was a simple instruction I thought you capable of."

"Then what were you doing there?" Martin asked firmly. "It was my understanding that you detested horse racing."

Artemis began to control his anger. If he was going to have to explain why he was there, then he had better do so with a clear head. The last thing he wanted to do was raise any suspicion in these two detectives, who, though might appear incompetent, were in fact shrewd operators.

Calmly he began to clarify the reason for his presence at Lingfield racecourse. It was down to his sister and her dream of beating the bookmakers. Trying to cajole him into accompanying her to Lingfield, she had presented him with a race card pointing to various horses which she thought could earn them a fortune. While she was babbling on, Artemis noticed that a Max Phillips was the owner of two horses that were due to race at the meeting.

His sister drove him in her usual reckless way to the track, all the while wearing a smug look. She had after all delivered a bit of a coup getting her little brother to go horse racing. Vaguely, Artemis pointed out a few horses which he assured Caroline were going to be winners.

"When she went to place her wagers with odd men standing on boxes, I wandered over to the owners' enclosure. They wouldn't let me in, then I saw you walk out of the bar with Max and his manservant. I was undecided as to the reason you were there. I presume you were asking him questions, or have you taken up socialising with old men?"

"I did want to ask him some questions." Susan went on to explain her visit to the house and Max's invitation to watch some races, she never passed up an opportunity for free drink and entertainment.

"I'm going to ask you if you found anything of interest, but first I must query if this is the way you normally live?" He looked around the kitchen. "I believed I lived in a sort of decorating flux, but this, well, am I witnessing some new fashion which all middle-class homes will be aspiring to? Don't tell me, shabby chic."

"Builders," Martin pointed out. "They started this morning, so just be thankful you visited tonight and not tomorrow, I understand it will only get worse."

"Very well, good luck with that one, builders are a law unto themselves. But Susan did you find out anything of interest?" He now sounded much more relaxed than when he had arrived.

Susan could not hide the look of superiority that covered her entire face as she recounted what she had learnt from Max during the afternoon.

Yes, Alan did have something that belonged to him. The old man was just as eager as they were to locate Alan, especially as his man had already learnt from Ian that the body on the floor was not Alan. She then added that she had obtained an address for a woman who appeared to be Alan's mistress.

Artemis accepted a glass of wine as Susan continued. This investigation was not going the way he had planned. All he had wanted was for the Hayden pair to make the link between Alan and Max. That was all. Provide some impartial evidence that the disappearance might be linked to Max. The last thing he wanted were two rogue private investigators digging deeper and deeper, yet he could not think of any way to stop them now that they had come this far. What he found difficult to believe was Max Phillips importing drugs and then selling them; that didn't seem like the sort of thing he would do. But who could tell, the temptation for easy money is strong.

"Mrs Hall, we assume is having an affair with her boss, the plumber. We now understand that Alan too was having an affair. More details to follow on that when you speak to her tomorrow." Artemis turned to Martin, "we know a bit more than we did; however, I still strongly believe this is now a matter for the police. Alan, as far as we can tell is alive. Therefore, I'll say again, I've no real interest in pursuing this matter.

"I would advise you, for the sake of your own safety, to step away from digging any deeper. The police are far better placed, better trained and have oodles of resources available to them. There's nothing to be gained if you continue."

He was expecting after that warning for Martin to be happy to conclude the whole thing, rein in his wife and step away from the issue. Martin just looked at Susan, he wasn't going to savour what he was about to say, but he knew what she was going to want.

"We'll continue. If you wish to stop paying us, that's fine, but we will be carrying on with this until we locate Alan."

"If that's the case, then I'll support you as best I can. But you must keep me informed without delay of any developments in the case."

Susan smiled at her husband, her mum had always said newlywedded men needed to be trained, Martin appeared to be responding well.

"So..." Susan started, ready to lay out her plans for the continuing investigation as well as ask Artemis about his personal life, only to be interrupted by the doorbell.

"Who on earth is that at this time of night?" Martin asked as he went towards the front door. He returned with their newest guest.

"Suzie baby, this is more like it, you're sitting at a table with a half-drunk bottle of wine, far better than shady cafés." Colin turned to Artemis, "well charming, if you're planning a threesome, you could have at least asked me first." Colin pushed his hand forward, ready to shake. "I'm Colin, senior fashion advisor to the Hayden family."

The two men shook hands, Artemis not sure what to say or make of Colin.

"You've gone red," Susan pointed out.

"Being a blonde was getting to be a little too tarty for me. I'm not getting any younger, so I took the plunge and I'm now a red head. Schwarzkopf Pillar Box Red to use its official title. Do you think it's a little too bright?"

"No, it's so you," Susan warmly confirmed. "Colin, this is Artemis, we're working with him on a case. Artemis, this is Colin."

"Are you a crossdresser?" Artemis asked remaining firmly seated at the table. He was still in a bit of a tetchy mood, Susan noticed; his often-relaxed demeanour had disappeared for some reason.

"I have a hairstyle very much associated with females. I'm wearing an attractive, highly patterned blouse over tight jeans that are tucked into knee-length boots. I also carry a handbag. So yes, I suppose I could be described as a crossdresser. In the same way, you look like a grown man wearing children's fashions. And your t-shirt! Status Quo didn't they stop touring decades ago? I think you should get yourself a new one.

"I presume I can join you all at the table and consume wine while you update me on the investigation." Without waiting for an answer, he sat down holding his hand out waiting for a glass.

"Ignore Colin," Susan told Artemis. "He might be an old crossdresser, but his experience in the police has helped us out on several occasions."

"He's your friend?" Artemis asked with an incredulous tone in his voice. The question was directed at Susan, but Martin answered it.

"Colin is our friend. The only downside with him is he does say it like it is."

"Exactly, like why I'm still waiting for a glass of wine to be put into my hand?"

As Susan updated Colin with Artemis adding the occasional extra snippet of information, Martin wondered if he would ever get to Verona. As he listened to the theories and counter-theories bouncing across the table, he was seriously wondering if the trip had a cancellation clause. Especially when Colin began to ask several new questions.

"Suzie baby, you were being a very naughty girl to visit Max Phillips, he's after all obviously up to no good. Also, what sort of key was it that was collected from the dead body? It's no doubt a key of value to someone. Was it a Yale?"

She didn't know. Colin suggested it would be a good idea to call the undertakers and see if she could get a description from the guy who had his eyes on the keyring.

"The main thing is you and hubby have a word with the mistress, see what she has to offer." Colin then turned to Artemis.

"There's another thing, well two actually," he added. "Alan's stolen bike, wasn't there an insurance claim for it?"

"Yes," Artemis retorted, "but it has no relevance to what has happened here."

"Oh, I think it does. Let me have the details of the theft. The second request I have is for a list of outgoing and incoming calls for Mrs Hall's mobile. That could reveal something interesting."

Having felt his professional reputation to be dented, Artemis asked about Colin's visit to the supermarket where

Mrs Hall and her boyfriend had gone, had he gleaned anything worthwhile?

"Top me up and I'll tell." Colin held his now empty glass towards Martin.

He had been lucky. Howard, the CCTV security guard at Tesco, had never worked with a detective dressed in women's clothes before, so he was happy to disregard any requirement under the data protection act. Together they examined the store CCTV footage from the time Mrs Hall and her lover had arrived.

It was easy, they saw her enter the store, pick up a basket then proceed to walk around the shop.

"The thing is, she bought nothing at all, she put the empty basket back as she left the store. The only thing she did was meet a man in the greeting card aisle, they chatted for maybe no more than a minute before parting. To be honest the angle was not great, the picture was not the highest of resolution, but I think there's a high chance the man could be..." He paused, he liked the dramatic effect, feeling the tension in his audience, waiting for the obvious. It was Susan who told him.

"Alan! She met her husband in the shop."

"Well done, Suzie baby, we'll make a detective out of you yet. He left soon after her, but as you know, there's just about zero camera coverage in the car park. But Mr and Mrs Hall do appear to be still talking, no doubt planning something, without the aid of an Ouija board."

Listening to Colin, Martin wondered just why he had not commented on the state of the kitchen. Having guests in the middle of a building site, made him feel a little embarrassed. He did intend to invite them into the living room, but once the wine started flowing, that thought was washed away by the alcohol.

"You haven't made any sharp comments about our kitchen," Martin said, echoing Susan's thoughts.

"To be honest, I decided against mentioning that your kitchen looks like a bomb's hit it. Suzie baby told me that you were getting into DIY and not loving it much. You've made a good start here, but I sense you might have taken on a little too much for your poor soft hands."

"I was talking about an IKEA construction kit upstairs," Susan pointed out. "This mess is professionally acquired; we have kitchen fitters doing their stuff."

"Oh, that's a relief, it's renewed my faith in Martin's incompetence and lack of ambition."

Chapter 18

The address Archie had secretly given Susan was on the Isle of Grain, close to the sprawling complex known as All Hallows Holiday Park. Susan remembered as a child she and her family had spent a whole week there in a six-berth caravan.

"It rained every day. Mum and Dad said that was the last time we were ever going to spend a holiday in England," Susan told Martin. "I think the following year we went to Spain, we weren't drowned, just burnt in the sun. I guess that's what holidays are all about, drama and distress."

Susan's experience was one of the reasons that All Hallows Holiday Park had remained a small, isolated resort facing the estuary of the River Thames. Conceived back in the 1930s when it seemed achievable, it was destined to be the best holiday resort in Europe. The new resort was to have the largest swimming pool in the UK, be full of innovation, including an artificial wave generator; the first in Europe. Not forgetting an amusement park four times the size of Blackpool's amusements, attracting millions of Londoners for their holidays. Building work started in 1937.

Then a global war interrupted the whole development, everything was put on hold. When peace resumed, cheap flights to the sun, the closure of the only railway line to the resort, plus the poor weather, was the final nail in the super resort. All plans and developer's dreams were abandoned.

Alan's mistress did not reside in the holiday park, which was still reserved for the few holiday makers who might be fearful of flying. She lived just off the High Street, in a crammed complex of caravans, mobile homes and run-down chalets. This residential park was for the exclusive use of the elderly, well over fifty-five at least. It was a place to retire and pass the final years of your life. Susan thought a week in a caravan with the rain bucketing down was bad enough.

Sylvia de Costa Williams, sounded like the Spanish beach where Susan was burnt to a cinder during her first foreign holiday. But Archie had assured her that really was the lady's name.

Avery Park Residential Homes was the last right turn at the end of a cul-de-sac. Plastered with no parking signs and residents only notices, it was not the most inviting place Martin had ever arrived at. Driving slowly along the pitted concrete road with its regular speed humps; they were looking for number 342. Everywhere they glanced there were other instructional signs: No ball games, No Dogs, Disabled Parking Only, Rubbish non-recyclable, Barbeques banned. Old people needed a lot of guidance, Martin thought.

Three hundred and forty-two was a large mobile home painted pink with a green roof. Along one side, decking protruded from the caravan. It had a neat balustrade with a gap in the middle to access the few steps that led towards the front door.

It was very neat, tidy, clean and well-kept, just like the lady who answered the door. Maybe in her sixties, tall, with well-defined facial features, smooth skin and just enough make-up to accentuate the shape of her face, without appearing plastered on. Dressed smartly in a very sensible blouse and jacket and a pencil skirt with a hemline modestly set just below her knee. She looked at her visitors with a frown before she spoke.

"If you're here about my dog, I no longer have it, it's with the Hoo Dog Rescue now. I would say they're pleased to obtain such a marvellous example of the breed. Are you happy now?"

"We're not here about the dog," Susan pointed out, "we're here to ask about Alan."

"Alan, ah, then you'd best come inside. Please wipe your feet as you enter. The grass has only recently been cut after a long hiatus, now there are clippings everywhere and the last thing I want is for you to walk them in."

Inside was equally neat, tidy and immaculately clean. It appeared everything had a place and was returned to its exact spot should it be moved for any reason. There was a fragrance of jasmine in the air. Sylvia sat in a large cushioned armchair, with a rose and cornflower pattern. Susan and Martin sat on the twin seater version opposite. She stared at them as if she was trying to read their minds, which indeed she was. Having practised white magic for the best part of two decades, she believed she could see into any of her guest's minds. She was actually delusional, but on occasions she had, by sheer chance, been lucky enough to pre-empt her guest's questions.

Already she had received a visit from a tall Asian man asking about Alan. She took an instant dislike to him, he was very smarmy, she thought. She had told him nothing, why should she, he was up to no good, she could tell. These two seemed a little more relaxed and appeared to be decent.

"We wanted to ask you about Alan and any contact you might have had with him over the last couple of weeks."

In white witch circles, her rightful place she believed, there was a rule that indicated that it's always better to keep your words to a minimum and listen to what others are saying. That way you were supposed to be able to delve into their minds with greater ease. However, Sylvia was not and had never been able to restrict the number of words that she spoke in any given reply.

"Why is it that recently everyone wants to know about Alan and my relationship. I always believed that an affair should be secret. He was married and we were close. Hence, I assumed the relationship to be undercover. I am now starting to understand that secret was not in Alan's vocabulary.

"First the Asian man who I didn't like. Not because of his colour, I could never be called a racist. But I didn't trust him one little bit. He wanted to know where he might find Alan. But you two look like a good-natured couple, so I might answer some of your questions."

Sylvia stood up, walked over to a burning candle, hence the jasmine fragrance engulfing the mobile home, genuflected towards the flickering flame before returning to her seat.

"I have, I will admit, seen Alan since his death. It was always clear to me that he would return during his passing. He stayed a while, but I haven't seen or heard from him in maybe a week or ten days. I'm surprised that there's such an interest in our relationship."

"Alan's not dead," Susan corrected.

"Oh, he is my dear, he is. He came to me one night; I was asleep, and he was knocking at the door. Poor boy, he was flustered and confused, quite normal for anyone passing through the veil of death towards the everlasting light of the next world. I calmed him."

"He's not dead," Susan repeated.

"I assure you he is. He told me, 'Sylvie', he always called me that, 'Sylvie, you must help me, everyone thinks I'm dead and I need to hide away for a few days.' Poor boy, he was so scared and confused, it's so understandable. Passing over to the other side can be daunting and I would guess terrifying if you're not prepared for the journey. He truly believed he was still alive. A common mistake for souls in transition."

Susan and Martin looked at each other, they instinctively knew what the other was thinking; 'What is she on about?' Not wishing to get into a debate about the current status of Alan's soul, Susan moved the conversation on.

"Did he hide away with you for a few days?"

"I told him, stay as long as you like. He was my lover, but you knew that all along. I'm readily admitting the fact as I have no reason to feel guilty about our love.

"He stayed for just over three days with me, finding comfort and reassurance as he waited to be drawn up to heaven and his final destination. During that time, we meditated a lot, revisited our interactions, and spoke of the future and how in time I might be alongside him, unless he reincarnates sooner than expected."

Martin had a lot of questions, most of which he thought were plainly stupid things to ask, yet he would have liked a few more details. First, he wanted to know if there was a time frame laid out for reincarnation. Not that he believed, but it was mildly interesting. He also wanted to know, was this mobile home on the Isle of Grain perchance God's waiting room, if so, had she had other visitors. As Martin pondered which question to ask first, he felt Sylvia's green eyes gaze towards him.

"Your aura tells me you are disbelieving. It's a frame of mind that isn't unexpected, especially with men. Even Alan, as he was beginning his journey between earth and heaven, wasn't convinced he was no longer of this physical earth."

Cynical Martin wanted to draw her attention to the fact that Alan was not actually dead. Sensibly he did not bring that to her notice, instead he asked a question. "What did he do here for those three days?" Instantly he regretted the question, thinking that he had already been told they were lovers, so what would lovers do for three days holed up in this prefab on wheels?

"We made love. It's the only earthly pleasure he could still enjoy. Although he was able to eat and drink, but I believe we can put that down to his fear of ascending to the spirit world, he was clinging onto earthly rituals."

Again, they looked at each other; 'What is she on about?'.

"Did he speak to anyone else while he was here?" Susan decided that although Sylvia might be on a different planet to most of the residents of this retirement park, Alan was very much in the land of the living.

"He did communicate via my mobile phone. He was only able to do that as I'm a white witch, with powers and skills which allowed his voice to be heard beyond the ether that was drawing him ever closer."

Good skill, Susan thought, just the sort of add on she could do with on her mobile which at times barely had a signal.

"Clearly he's now passed over to the other side," Susan observed, assuming there were just the three of them in the mobile home, and Sylvia had not crammed a gang of heavenly spirits into the wardrobe. That did raise another question in Susan's mind, what were a group of ghosts called, apart from scary. That problem would have to wait for another day, things were confused enough as they were.

"You're a Leo, young lady, aren't you?"

Susan smiled. "Spot on, making me: creative, passionate, generous, warm-hearted, cheerful, humorous. I could go on."

"I was more leaning towards the negative trait of being inflexible. You should accept that the road to heaven is a two-way street."

"When did he leave?" Susan asked bluntly, noticing her husband was stifling a laugh.

Sylvia admitted that Alan had passed through the gateway on his journey to spiritual enlightenment more than a week ago. She was confident that she would hear from him again once he had settled into his new surroundings. Martin tried to bring the white witch back down to Earth.

"Do you know who he might have called?"

"No. It's sacrosanct for me to remain ignorant as to who he was speaking to, they were after all going to be his last earthly words, it's only right they should be confidential. However, I did check my phone afterwards. There were no numbers listed, it had indeed been a spiritual telephone conversation, proving he was dead."

They drove away. In the rear-view mirror, Martin could see Sylvia de Costa Williams waving goodbye, her hand gliding through the air as if she was on another planet. They both agreed the visit had been a total waste of time, although Susan did point out that if it turned out that Alan had died at some point between leaving the Frenchman on the floor and arriving at Sylvia's, they would have to eat their words.

"Meeting a white witch has reminded me that I haven't read your stars today." Before she could get to the webpage on her phone and much to Martin's relief, Susan had an incoming call.

Chapter 19

As they were driving back to see Mrs Hall, Susan took two phone calls. The first from Pete the undertaker. As best as he could recall there were two keys, a Yale and one for a mortice lock. Apart from the Ferrari key fob that he was interested in, there was one of those cheap plastic fobs that held a small label. What was written on the label, he did have a bit of a clue. He remembered it as 'Farts Holiday Park'. He was the first to admit that it wasn't the real name, but he could remember that he was looking at it and thinking that it was a strange name for a holiday park. All he could say was that the real name must sound like fart: Bart, Heart, Mart, Chart. What he did recollect was the number on it, which was either 66 or 99, depending on which way you looked at it.

Politely Susan thanked him, it was not much, but better than nothing. Martin was not so sure, "How many thousands of holiday homes are there in the country? Even if you only look at the ones with 'art' in the title, there must still be a few hundred."

"Look on the bright side, when we find it there are only two numbers to choose from," Susan replied.

Her second call was from Artemis. After Colin's request, he had obtained a list of incoming and outgoing calls for the mobile of Mrs Hall. By his own admission the list made interesting reading. A large number of calls to her boss, more than one might imagine would be deemed as normal. The inference he was making was obvious, another question for Susan to ask Mrs Hall. Then there were a few calls from a Sittingbourne number, 01795, all incoming.

"I'm trying to identify a name and address for that number, but as ever these things take time. I'll call you as soon as I have one."

"Maybe Mrs Hall will help us," Susan suggested to Martin as she explained the details of the call. "Right, star time, let's see what you Pisces have in store today."

"You don't have to," Martin offered, a proposal Susan refused to acknowledge and began his horoscope for the day.

"'Your progress can be measured by other people's reactions today'. I wonder how Mrs Hall will react when we turn up. 'Avoiding conflict should be your goal'. Little chance of that is there. 'The good news is that you have someone who can help you. Turn to him or her when you feel yourself faltering'. Always told you I was your best support, when you trip up, I'll catch you. 'You may not be able to sing a solo, but you still get the most of the applause'. Typical bloke, we girls do all the work and you lot get all the praise."

"I can't argue with that, after all it's in the stars," Martin chuckled.

Chapter 20

They were the last people Mrs Hall wanted to see on her doorstep again. She knew that she was about to be subjected to a list of difficult questions which were becoming more and more problematic to answer. Even so she smiled politely and invited them in, with the caveat that they could not stay long as she was about to go to work.

"I wish I could start work after lunch," Susan said looking at her boss, a comment that was either lost or ignored by him.

Christine Hall explained that she was still on reduced hours, a concession that her boss was happy to allow given the complex situation she had found herself in. Graciously she sat down and asked them the reason for yet another visit.

She wants to get to the point, Martin thought, so he obliged.

"You recall the last time we were here, we talked about the accident your boss had in the car park while you were shopping. What did you buy?"

"What's that got to do with anything? How does my buying biscuits for the office contribute to the two of you finding the body of my husband?"

"It would help us clear up a little misunderstanding," Martin sounded calm. He had all the cards in his hand, he just wanted to see her bluff as best she could.

"I told you, supplies for the office, you know the normal sorts of things, tea, coffee, biscuits, milk, plus some herbal teas. Don't ask me what brand and types of biscuits because I don't recall. I have had much bigger things on my mind, as you know," her voice had shifted from the reasonable and polite to a more hostile tone.

"But you left empty handed," Martin responded to her explanation.

Without missing a beat, she replied vigorously, "That would be because I had left my credit cards in the car. And before you ask, when I got back to the car, Manny, my boss, said we didn't have time, he needed to get back to the shop."

Susan took up the questioning, for no better reason than Martin's stars said he should avoid conflict and she guessed the next question would generate a few fireworks from Christine Hall.

"Who was the man you spoke to in the greeting card aisle at Tesco?" Although Susan tried to keep a straight face, she could not help just the faintest grin. Her question sounded like something out of a slushy romance novel.

"He was asking my advice on buying a card for his wife. I offered my thoughts and he seemed pleased. Who'd you think he was?"

"Well, not your husband, he's dead, isn't he? Although I can't imagine why you were hanging around the birthday card section when you were buying biscuits." Susan did not wait for an answer before her next question. "How well do you know your boss?" Susan watched Christine tense up, the question and all its implications were not lost on Alan's wife.

"As well as any employee knows their boss. Manny, as I've told you before, has been good to me through a very difficult time, very supportive. My husband was never reassuring, and no doubt he had other interests and diversions in his life."

"Was Manny the friend you were staying with the night Alan was meant to have died?"

The reaction to Susan's question was immediate, Christine spoke sharply, "Why are we going over the same questions time and time again. I've already told you, the night Alan died I was in Crawley, with an old school friend, working on her garden."

Christine was now tense, very tense, even Martin could see it. She was almost squirming in her seat waiting for the next predictable question. Susan liked to be unpredictable at times, it worked wonders on TV shows, she hoped it did the same in real life.

"We think Alan might still be alive. On the run, having got into trouble with a drug dealer."

Christine took a moment to absorb that suggestion, she was not so concerned about defending Alan, more herself and her position.

"That sentence is the most absurd I've heard in a long while. My husband is dead; it's just his body that's unaccounted for. As for drug dealing, I've heard nothing so outlandish in my life. I know Alan was happy to do a bit of ducking and diving, losing the odd air conditioning unit for a private client. But drugs, no way would he ever get involved in such a thing."

"It's just a theory we're working on," Susan pointed out with a smile, before she asked outright, "When I said who was the friend you stayed with, I was referring to the days after your husband's alleged death. The companion that you stayed with then, I'm guessing that was Manny, your kind and considerate boss."

"I've had enough of you two with your stupid questions and wild theories. I think you'd better leave now; I've got work to do."

Christine stood up, making it clear that it was time for them to vacate her house, which they did without complaint.

They were now convinced beyond a shadow of a doubt that Christine and her boss were lovers. If she was not going to admit it out loud, they wondered if Manny might. Colin had planned to visit the plumber's shop at the same time they were with Christine, a strategy he described as a classic pincer movement.

As Christine was about to close the front door, Susan turned and asked one final question, "Who do you know in Sittingbourne that would call you several times?"

"No one. Goodbye." The door slammed shut.

Susan smiled; she had learnt so much about detecting from watching TV programmes about them. All she was missing now was a shabby raincoat and a Basset Hound.

Chapter 21

Regular customers at Sane Sanitation Plumbing Supplies had never seen anything so crazy. The constant flow of plumbers through the doors brought a range of body shapes, dressing in a selection of unfashionable styles. Fat plumbers who wore shorts no matter the weather. Thin plumbers preferred dark t-shirts with work-stained body warmers. Then there were those who wore expensive trainers and matching track suit bottoms and tops. If you wore branded clothes to work, then you must be doing all right.

Today Colin walked through the automatic door of the plumbers' merchants and at once added a new level to the fashion stakes. Dressed in jeans, with sensible court shoes sporting a gold buckle. It was a chilly day, so he was warmly wrapped in an insulated padded jacket, in a fetching shade of dusty pink, which co-ordinated well with his bright-red dyed hair. His make-up was nothing special, he was, after all, working.

"Are you a poof?" asked one confused plumber who was leaving the shop with a white toilet seat under his arm.

Colin slowly looked the questioner up and down before concluding, "By poof I assume you mean a gay man, no I'm not, and even if I was, I wouldn't fancy you in the least. Don't be disappointed, I'm sure you and your toilet seat will find true love in the end." That brought hoots of laughter from the other customers, which encouraged the man with the toilet seat to leave quickly.

"But you're a bloke?" This time the question came from behind the counter.

"Yes, indeed I am. I'm a gender non-conforming person, if my attire confuses you. I'm here to see Emmanuel Prendergast who by the looks of that tattoo on your finger must be you."

All eyes now turned towards the tall thin man behind the counter. A short customer in jeans and a torn checked shirt remarked, "Emmanuel! No wonder you prefer Manny."

"I do prefer Manny for obvious reasons. What can I do for you?" he asked Colin who was now leaning on the counter examining a small display of screwdrivers.

"I need to ask some personal questions which I think you'd prefer to answer out of ear shot of this motley bunch. I'll just say it's connected with a minor traffic accident you were involved in at Tesco."

"And who are you exactly?"

"Fair question. I'm working for the insurance company. I presume you have a private office on the premises."

Manny led Colin behind the counter, through a congested stockroom into a small office, which was clogged with boxes and an insignificant desk overloaded with piles of papers.

"I'd offer you a seat, but there's only the one and I hope this won't take too long. I told you guys at the time I wasn't bothered in the least about the damage, it was the other driver who had a fit of honesty come over her. Too much paperwork to worry about for a bit of paint."

"You and Christine getting it on is more of an interest to me."

The atmosphere in the room darkened in an instant. Manny walked behind the desk and sat down on the worn-out swivel chair. Nervously he swung himself from side to side. "What's any of that got to do with an insurance company?"

"Husband has gone missing, people, not me you understand, start to ask questions. Wife and lover conspiring to get rid of the husband? Silly question, but people do ask such things. Any chance of a cup of tea, I'm spitting feathers and gather we'll be having a long conversation?"

"We don't have the space here, the café right next door does fine for us. I have an account there; special customers get to have hospitality on it, which helps trade. But we're not going next door to talk about me and Christine. As this should be a short conversation."

"Well, I'm listening." Colin leaned against the door frame, tempted though he was to sit on the desk, but thought it would look weird even for him.

"What do you want to know?"

"The five W's. What do you know about his disappearance? Where is Alan currently staying? Why did he want to vanish off the face of the earth? Who gains by his death? When are you going to understand that the game's up?"

Emmanuel Prendergast, at the ripe old age of thirty, had spent six years getting his hands dirty down other people's toilets, fixing their leaks and overall getting fed up. Being a plumber was not all it was made out to be. What he did see, was that plumbers needed to have supplies, so why not sit in a warm, clean shop and sell all those plumbers their materials. A lot easier than installing hot water tanks in dusty cobweb-filled lofts.

The shop was a success. He knew marketing, he knew plumbers, the profits continued to rise. He then employed a woman a little older than him to keep up to date with the accounts. Christine was attractive, helpful, and seemed to like him. He had not had much time for any sort of relationship, but he started to build one with Christine knowing full well she was married. She had made it clear at the very start that her marriage to Alan was empty and going nowhere.

"The plan was for her to put in for a divorce, she had mentioned the subject to her husband, and he seemed to accept that their relationship was long past its sell by date. Proceedings had not been started, but we were all moving along that path. Then he seemingly dies, which at first seemed a godsend. Then the wrong body in the coffin complicated matters, apparently, you can't divorce a missing man.

"I guess you know by now he's alive. I don't know where, but he's after money from Christine. He wants just a quarter of the house value, then he'll be gone. Well, I talked to her about it, I could raise the cash, we could give it to him, then he would be out of our hair. We could move in together and live happily ever after."

Colin was tempted to wipe a tear from his eye, such was the rose-coloured story he was being told. The thing was Colin believed every word; Emmanuel meant everything that he said. It was as if he wanted to get a lot of issues off his chest. Maybe it helped, talking to a cross-dresser in a cramped office that resembled a confessional.

"Why didn't he just come back and get half the house in a divorce settlement."

"Well, if you find him, best ask him. I suspect the fact he found a body somewhere and gave it his name might be something that's holding him back from reappearing."

"Have you paid him off?"

"Can't get that sort of money in cash, there are rules. Until he can give me a bank account that he's got access to, we're in a Catch-22 position."

Chapter 22

Bill Latham had never married. He could not see the point of being a part of such a tradition. The only thing he had ever loved were his motorbikes. Preferably ones from the sixties and seventies, lots of chrome, noise, speed, and more importantly, built in the United Kingdom, not imported from Japan.

It was that romantic image of freedom which Bill liked. All the bikes he had ever owned were built before he was born. His favourite was the Norton Commando, introduced in 1967 and quickly became one of the most popular bikes of the era. It was powered by a parallel-twin engine and featured an innovative frame design that helped to reduce vibration. He had purchased his Norton Commando as a barn-find. Then he spent three years and a lot of hard-earned cash to restore the bike to showroom condition.

At the bottom of his garden was his purpose-built workshop. There he spent hours meticulously caring for his collection of bikes. Apart from the Norton, he had a road worthy Triumph Bonneville and a Velocette Venom; the latter he regularly took out onto the roads. His current project was rebuilding a BSA Gold Star, a classic British sports bike that was popular in the 1950s and 1960s. It was known for its high performance and was a favourite with road racers, not that Bill was planning to go racing, it was just a prestigious bike to own.

When he heard the doorbell from the workshop, it was a long trek up the garden, through the kitchen then along the hall to the front door. Hence, he had installed a camera doorbell, allowing him to converse with whoever was at the door. Not that he had many visitors, the most common person to stand on his doorstep was the DHL delivery man, who had got to know him well and semi-followed his restoration work.

Today he trudged up the garden, told his visitors to wait, he was coming. It gave him time to think. The investigators, how much did they know? How little could he say and get away with?

Bill Latham sat in the kitchen with his unwelcome guests. He half-listened to Martin and Susan, as he wiped his greasy hands on a plain tea-towel he kept for such occasions. He declined to offer them any sort of refreshment; he didn't want them in his house a moment longer than necessary.

As he answered their questions, he discarded the towel, throwing it towards the sink. It struck several discarded polystyrene cartons, he had feasted on a Turkish take away last night before spending hours in his workshop, tending his beloved bikes.

He was happy to share all he knew about Alan and his wife. He had listened to Alan on many occasions talking about their planned separation. They had never reached the dizzy heights of marital bliss that every romcom book or Mills and Boon painted as the ultimate in a relationship.

He sounded pleased to hear that Alan was alive when Martin told him. He had to look surprised, to be anything else would have given the game away.

Now they were asking questions which required a little more thought. Alan helping the import of contraband. This question needed a dose of imagination to answer.

"It's true, I did ask Alan to be a worker at Potts Field. He was a good bloke that I knew from the motorcycle club. He needed a job, and I could offer him one." That reply Bill was sure would put him in a good light, make him seem almost charitable.

"To be honest," he told Susan who had asked the question, "I did know occasionally a plane would land after dark when the airfield was closed, but Alan dealt with it all. He would ask me to stay in the portacabin while he spoke to the pilot. Who was I to ask questions? He would go off for a while, then I would hear the plane taking off and Alan would return, put the kettle on, and pass the whole thing off as a case of an incompetent pilot. He never mentioned anything more to me and I wasn't going to press him. Alan was a good bloke; his word was more than enough for me. If there was something underhand, well, I was more than happy not to be a part of it. The less I knew the better, that's how I saw things."

"Do you have any idea why Alan might want to disappear?" Susan asked.

What sort of a stupid question is that Bill thought. Doesn't everyone at some time or other want to disappear. Leave the mundane working life for a better life of relaxation, total freedom, throw off the shackles of monetary imprisonment.

"It was a shock," Bill admitted. "I had no idea, not even the slightest hint that he was going to jump off the world. When I first heard about him being found dead, I was sad, obviously. He was a mate, a good mate. Then to hear that his body wasn't in the coffin, well, beggars' belief. Now you're trying to tell me he's alive, hiding out someplace, that's the stuff of fiction."

They next asked if Alan had a caravan anywhere. Bill started to believe they knew a lot more than he had hoped they might. It was bad enough for them to be sitting in his kitchen telling him that they knew, not thought or assumed, but in reality knew Alan was alive. How the hell did they find that out? Now they were asking about a caravan, where one might be. Of course, Bill denied any knowledge. That was the best approach, deny, deny, deny. There were thousands of caravans in Kent let alone the rest of the country, they would have their work cut out finding the right one.

Now questions about a mistress, that was an easy one.

"Yes, Alan told me about his Sylvie. I think to be honest they did have something between them. He often talked about her in that tone of voice which made him sound like a love-struck schoolboy. I know she was older than him, but where love is concerned age is irrelevant, or so I'm told. Never been one for romance myself."

"You're a biking person," Martin pointed out. "We've heard that when his bike was stolen, he was more than a little upset about it. Was he that fond of an everyday bike?"

Ah, Bill thought, there you have it. The stolen bike. Everything was going so well up until that point. Why Alan was so desperate to fill up the tank at that time of night, Bill could not imagine. A tatty Yamaha MT-125 motorbike, which Alan used to commute between the airfield and his home. Bill would not have given the machine the time of day, but Alan thought it serviceable. But why fill up when you had no need to? Ever since the bike had been taken off the forecourt while Alan was paying cash for the petrol, nothing had gone right. Bill could say categorically that the moment the bike was taken, the whole arrangement began to crumble and fall. Although he could, he had no intention of telling these two.

"He just loved the bike. I think it hurt his pride; it being taken from under his nose," was all Bill said on the subject.

It was at that point the lady detective's phone rang. Bill didn't glean much from the side of the conversation he heard, yet whatever she had been told must have been important. They simply thanked him for his time and left in a hurry.

Just to be cautious, Bill made an urgent telephone call. He would now have to make some tricky decisions.

Chapter 23

"Hart's Holiday Park, Leysdown on the Isle of Sheppey is where the calls to Mrs Hall's phone came from. A phone box on the site. Well, it does rhyme with farts," Susan acknowledged with a smile.

Martin looked confused. "That's a long way to go. Should we take the car on the ferry or go as foot passengers?" he asked, genuinely concerned that he was going on an extended road trip to a place he had never been.

"What are you going on about a ferry for? They have a bridge. You know the sort cars can drive over."

"Oh, I'm sorry," the sarcasm was obvious, "I've never been to the Isle of Sheppey. I've read all about it, the Needles and the coloured sand, once an old aunt of mine gave me a glass tube of the stuff after she had stayed there."

"You dipstick, Martin, you should really try and get a refund on your expensive education. You're thinking of the Isle of Wight. We're going to the Isle of Sheppey; an hour down the road and over the bridge. Plus, a lot more down market I can assure you."

As they drove towards Leysdown, Susan was interested just what Martin thought of Bill Latham. For the most part he agreed with her, that he was being very cagey and on the whole implausible. Why, Martin argued, would you stand by as a plane landed in the dark, clearly not the sort of thing that should be happening, and then accept that there was nothing to worry about.

"Who did he think Alan was meeting? His mate popping in for a quick chat once in a while?"

Martin also concluded that Alan appeared to be the sort of man everyone trusted and took at his word. "It would seem to be the natural response, if Alan says so, it's fine."

The entrance to Hart's Holiday Park was off Leysdown High Street, at the end of a row of seaside-themed shops providing takeaway food, sweet treats and any number of plastic buckets and inflatable animals.

They drove in, there was no sign of any security or barriers to cross, they just trundled down a well-laid private road, with caravans six deep on either side.

Caravan sixty-six was a short walk into the orderly lines of holiday homes, which had no access to parking. If you had booked that number for your holiday, you would have had a bit of a route march with your luggage to get to your accommodation, which Susan assured Martin was all part of the caravanning experience. Once they had located sixty-six, which for some reason was sandwiched between fifty-eight and seventy-two, they immediately realised it was unlikely to be where Alan was staying. The doors of the caravan were open, three young children were playing outside and a man whose beer belly gave the impression he was pregnant, lay asleep in a deckchair, being in total dereliction of his duty watching over the children.

Even so, they disturbed him to make sure.

"Ain't no Alan here, just me 'n me missus, Gloria."

It would have to be ninety-nine, which was inserted between ninety-three and one hundred and five.

"The numbers go up and down and not across," Martin pointed out. "See my education was not a total waste of time." Susan did not bother to reply, she knew the true value of his education from previous experiences.

It was a grey-green caravan, large with a panoramic window at the front. The net curtains were drawn back on each window; whoever might be living here was not worried about being seen inside. It looked a spacious caravan, but the colour was dull and dreary, giving it the look of a beached Naval vessel.

They knocked on the door. Waited. Then knocked again. Susan peered through the windows.

"Well, someone is obviously living in there, and on the whole they're messy, so that'd be a bloke, I guess. But not in currently."

"We could wait a while," Martin suggested.

"Or grab some fish and chips and come back later." Susan's stomach was complaining about its lack of attention.

"Really, fish and chips?"

"Come on, we're at the seaside, what else is there to eat? Unless you've taken a sudden liking to whelks and winkles."

"God, no thank you; I'll suffer fish and chips."

Then another voice joined their conversation. The source was an old man who had emerged from the caravan behind ninety-nine. Although Martin was not really sure how you might define from behind or at the side of, when the caravan was surrounded by other caravans on all sides.

He guessed the park owners would have some system of working that one out.

"If you're looking for Alan, he's gone out to grab some supplies." The old man, who had now stepped away from his caravan, was moving towards Martin and Susan with a leery grin.

It was not exactly a hot day, even so the man walking towards them was dressed in just a pair of very tight speedo swimming trunks and flip flops. His leathery skin was very darkly tanned.

"Has he been gone long?" Susan asked, trying to avoid staring at his trunks, although there was not much to see.

"He'll be here soon enough; he's picking up some sausages." The man's voice had a lilting tone to it, not local, possibly Cornish, Susan thought. She was glad Colin was not with them today, he would have made at least one inappropriate comment about the man's attire.

They thanked him, adding that he need not mention that they had called.

"Always guessed he was a wanted man." Laughing he turned away and walked back to his caravan.

Chapter 24

Late afternoon in Leysdown is not the best time to sit down and eat fish and chips. The lunchtime rush had finished and the restaurants had now closed. The only option were the takeaways. Martin predictably refused to eat anything out of paper while walking along the street, however keen Susan might have been. The result was he found himself at a small round chrome-topped table at the Sheppey Bakery, nursing a cup of weak coffee and digging his teeth into a pasty that had been left on the shelf under the heating lamp for too long. Susan, whose culinary expectations were in general lower than his, eagerly consumed a chicken tikka roll, washing it down with a Pepsi Cola, which she drank straight from the can.

"We'll have this and then pop along to the amusements, spend a few quid on the machines. I used to love days out at the seaside with my sisters. There was just so much to do: digging in the sand, splashing in the water, eating fish and chips plastered with heaps of salt and vinegar. Then we'd all get five pounds each to spend how we liked in the amusements. I would spend all my money on those Penny Falls machines, willing the coin that I rolled down the ramp would end up perfectly placed to push a mountain of coins down the gap into the tray, where I could scoop my winnings up."

"Never really did the seaside," Martin admitted, leaving the rock-hard crust of his pasty on the side of his plate. "Our holidays were in Italy, spent in the main by the pool. Then days out were cultural stuff, galleries or the theatre. During my teenage years, a group of us popped down to Brighton a couple of times, but by then we were setting our sights on walking into a pub and getting served with alcohol, which in the main worked well. Freddie the Frog always looked older than a teenager.

"One thing I'm still waiting for is an answer about your interest in horse racing. You were about to explain when we were interrupted. Where does all your knowledge come from?"

"It's really no big deal, Martin, it's just one of life's lessons you pick up."

"No, it's not. There must be more to it than just casual interest."

"Alright, but I don't want you getting mad or annoyed. Promise?"

"How bad can it be?"

As the youngest sister, Susan explained, she had a habit of following her older siblings' lead to appear grown up. She looked upon them through rose-tinted glasses, wanted to be as mature as they were, which was the most annoying habit of any younger brother or sister. Although she thought horses overall pretty boring, the fact that her sisters pleaded with their parents to get them a horse, she followed them.

There was a shortage of conventional horse stables near the family home in Tooting, but her father did have a useful contact, who held a sort of managerial position at a stables on the outskirts of London, a short train ride away.

This meant every Saturday the three Morris sisters would jump on a bus, pick up a train from Clapham Junction and attend Castle Farm Stables just outside Guildford. Looking back, Susan now understood that her parents probably took full use of the free time their children's absence presented.

At first Susan was not convinced that mucking out a horse stable was an efficient use of her time away from school, but her older sisters seemed to enjoy it, so Susan decided she would have to like it as well.

She took more interest in the gambling aspects than the horse-keeping part of her job. Talking to trainers and jockeys, it became a thrill to see one of the horses that she worked with win a race.

Her fascination for the sport continued and as her sisters grew older and took more notice of boys and fashion, it was left to her to travel to Castle Farm Stables every Saturday, continuing the tradition her older siblings had started.

Now in her late teens and such a part of the stables, Susan was invited to local racecourses to help look after the horses prior to and after their races. Lingfield, Sandown and Ascot, she knew them all intimately. The excitement as well as the responsibility was something she enjoyed. It was during this time that she began to understand race-form. How racehorses developed, how some liked the ground hard, some liked the going soft. It was nothing like academic studies at school, a place where she hated to learn and could not see the point. But without realising, she was putting the maths and physics she had learnt to good use.

"You volunteered to clean out horse muck from a stable? There must have been another incentive to go out in the country and be an unpaid stable girl," Martin pointed out.

"There was, I will admit, but I'm coming to that." Susan was not going to be rushed, she wanted Martin to learn about this part of her life armed with all the facts.

"The reason I chose to help out at Castle Farm stables was simple..."

"Excuse me," a voice interrupted her monologue. They looked up at the man, who was now standing beside their table with a wistful look in his eyes. "I believe you're looking for me."

Chapter 25

Looking around Alan's caravan, Martin wondered how he and Sylvia had ever managed to be together for more than a few hours, let alone a few days, after his hypothetical death. It had very much the look of the airfield portacabin: a chaotic mess. Although Martin reasoned that just like the portacabin, he was sure Alan could put his hands on anything he wanted quickly and effortlessly. In his chaos, everything had a place.

They sat on a semi-comfortable cushioned bench that was fitted on one side of the caravan, continued under the large panoramic window with draping net curtains, then continued still further around, forming a U-shape. Alan sat opposite his invited guests, who had refused the offer of a beer, which did not stop him drinking a lager straight from the bottle.

It was a strange experience for Martin. Over the last few days, he had learnt a lot about the life and death of Alan Hall. He had seen his photograph, talked to his wife, his friends, his colleagues, knew about the night shifts he did, and those he, with the cooperation of his fellow workers, avoided. Martin knew a lot about Alan, now for the first time he was seeing him in the flesh.

He was taller than he had imagined, for some reason he had always assumed Alan to be on the slightly short side. He was not overweight, just physically sound, a manual worker. In fact, he was tall and thin with a pale complexion, which might have arisen from claiming to be dead and avoiding being caught in the land of the living.

"I guess an explanation might be in order."

"Well," Susan started, sounding like a mother who was about to give her teenage son a dressing down after catching him smoking in his bedroom. "I think that would be the least you can do given the amount of distress your fictional death has caused, as well as the inconvenience to ourselves having to chase around all the places you frequent."

"In that case, for you to fully understand just why I wanted to disappear, I'd better start at the point things began to go badly wrong for me."

***

Alan took them back to the petrol station. He mostly used his motorbike to travel between home and his place of work, unless the weather was really bad, then he would use his car. He had popped out from work to run an errand, on the way deciding that it would be prudent to fill up with petrol. He didn't need to; it was just there had been talk in the media about an up-and-coming strike by petrol tanker drivers.

As he was paying, the cashier saw someone jump on his bike and ride off. He ran out and chased the teenager across the forecourt but stood no chance of catching him. His bike was gone. It had happened so quickly. The cashier phoned the police, offered CCTV footage, overall they had been very helpful. As were the police, but the bike was gone and they did not hold much hope of finding it, or the rider, with his hoodie and scarf on there was little chance of him being recognised.

"I knew there that night, talking to the police, learning I'd not get my bike back, that life was going to change dramatically for me. And before you ask, I need to take you back a bit further in time. Soon after I'd joined Bill working on night shift at Pott's Field.

"I'd only been there a matter of days. Bill had offered me the job knowing I was looking around for something. I had known Bill for a couple of years, we had an interest in motorbikes, although he was the aficionado in that department, I just liked riding fast.

"Well, as I said, I had only been there a matter of days when Bill explains to me that occasionally a plane will land while we're on shift. I ask him, how's that work, it's pitch black out there, how does a plane land? He explained that he stands at the top edge of the runway – well it's more of a flat field really – and he wanted me to stand at the bottom edge. We would both hold torches and when he put his on, I'd put mine on. The plane somehow sees the lights and drops down and lands. Bill said it was a bit like during the war when RAF planes landed behind enemy lines with spies and stuff."

He stood up, took off his jumper, which he threw down beside him and then finished his beer, before returning to his seat and continuing his story.

"I asked why it lands, and Bill said, the pilot drops off a package and we just need to deliver it to someone and get a handsome profit from it. How much, I asked, well, I wanted to know because it sounded dodgy to say the least. A grand between us. That was useful cash to have. Five hundred quid to hold a torch and drop off a package, no questions asked. Of course, I was in."

Alan continued with a description of the first landing he encountered. He stood like a lemon in the darkness at one end of the runway, then when he saw Bill's large torch illuminate, he followed suit. A few minutes later, he heard the drone of a propeller driven aircraft coming closer and closer, then it passed over his head nearer than he would have liked and saw the dark shadowy plane bounce along the runway.

As instructed, he waited. It was five minutes at most before Bill turned on his torch again. Alan followed suit and heard the ever-increasing sound of an aeroplane coming towards him. That first time, he was terrified the plane was going to hit him. It didn't but he felt the downdraught as it flew off over his head and up into the night.

Back in the portacabin, he found Bill holding a packet a little bigger than a shoe box. He had a big smile. 'Right, you stay here, I'll be back in about an hour'. Alan did exactly that and Bill returned as promised.

But the money, Bill explained to Alan, would get paid later in the week and to prove that he was on the level and not going to fiddle his mate, Alan could pick up the cash by meeting a bloke at a restaurant.

"I had to wait until this tall Asian guy went to the toilet, after that, I should go. There was no rush, but I liked to go in soon after him. There, behind the drawer in the sink unit, was a wad of notes which I stuck in my pocket. One thousand pounds exactly, Bill was being straight as a die with me. If a bloke is honest with cash, he's a top geezer in my book."

"But you guessed whatever you were doing was illegal?" Susan asked, to confirm Alan was not convincing himself that such action was typical of a night crew at an airport.

"Didn't want to know. If you don't ask questions, you don't get lied to. For all I knew there could have been Milk Tray chocolates in the box."

"Then how does this tie into your bike being stolen and you wanting to appear dead?" Martin asked, struggling to keep track, although he did feel some satisfaction about working out the way Alan was paid in the restaurant.

Alan asked for their tolerance as he continued his story, which would in the end answer all their questions.

Over the next few weeks, he explained, a plane landed mostly once a week, but sometimes there would be two deliveries, which occasionally meant they needed to switch shifts with the other crew, to ensure it was them around when the plane landed, normally about 10pm.

Between the two of them they developed a routine. Bill normally dropped off the parcel and Alan collected the cash. The main reason they chose that division of responsibilities was that Bill hated Turkish food. Occasionally he would let Alan deliver the parcel, to ensure both could, if need be, cover each other.

"So now and again I'd drop the parcel off at this big house where the Asian lived. Recognised him from the restaurant as soon as he opened the door. Wasn't that talkative, just grunted, took the parcel, and closed the door. But everything changed the night my bike was stolen."

That fateful night, he recalled, following the plane that had landed, Bill was deep into replacing a coil on one of his vintage bikes. He asked Alan to pop the parcel across. Happily, he set off with the parcel, a bit bigger than a breakfast cereal packet in the tail box on his bike.

"Did you fill up before or after dropping off the parcel?" Susan asked, even though in the back of her mind she knew the answer.

The parcel was still in the tail box when the thief drove off the garage forecourt and into the night. This left him without a bike and, more importantly, without the parcel that had just been imported into the country under the cover of darkness. They discussed what could be done but came up with nothing other than an admission to the man that the parcel had gone missing.

"Give him his due, Bill came with me to see the Asian guy. We told him what had happened at the doorstep and then he invited us in. For the first time I was inside the house, well posh, lots of nice stuff around. It turned out that the Asian guy was a type of bodyguard for the fat white bloke who was the boss man.

"Thankfully, although he dressed too loud for my taste, he was calm when we told him that his parcel had gone missing. All he asked of us was either track down who stole the bike and get the parcel and its contents back or compensate him for the loss.

"Now at that point I thought, alright, no chance of getting the parcel back, we'll have to make good the loss. 'How much? I asked' 'Three hundred thousand,' he said. Well, no way was I going to get that sort of cash. He then became a little more forceful, 'Oh yes that's the price, you'll find a way of paying me back.'"

"Well, to cut a long story short, we had little choice, it wasn't as if we could go to the police, or the insurance company and say, oh by the way there was something valuable in the bike, can I now claim for it."

"What do you think was in the parcel?" Susan wanted to know if she had guessed right.

"To be honest, at the time I never knew, Bill and I assumed it was drugs. Whatever, the old bloke wanted us to pay him three hundred grand. We didn't have that sort of money. Over the next couple of weeks, we tried to come up with some way of getting it. Additional mortgages, plus what savings we had only amounted to a half of what he wanted. We were stuck, still working for the old man, but nevertheless stuck and being a lot more careful with the parcels that continued to arrive.

"You sure you don't want a beer?" Alan asked as he went across the small space to the fridge and took another one for himself. As he came back Martin raised the matter of why he was handing himself in now.

"Let me finish my story and you'll see."

Certainly one for the dramatic effect, Martin thought.

Then another calamity befell the two conspirators. Bill came off his bike and was unable to work. Alan needed another person, a trustworthy one, to hold the other torch. The role fell to Alan's best friend, Ian, who was happy to do exactly as he was told, not tell anyone else and in general be the perfect partner in crime, for which he was well rewarded.

"It had to be perhaps during the second week that Ian was with me. The plane came in. I was now in the role of taking the parcel off the pilot. That night, the same as he ever did, he got out, handed the parcel across, walked to the portacabin, had a pee, then returned to his plane and off he goes. I never knew exactly where he had flown from, I didn't really care.

"He was walking back having relieved himself, lighting up a cigarette when he said something in a foreign language. I didn't know what he was saying but I saw him drop his lighter, grab his chest, stagger forward and then fall on the floor. It was as if he had just fallen asleep, but he hadn't, he was dead, which put me in a bit of a predicament."

Hearing a commotion Ian had left his post at the end of the runway to see what was happening. Between them they knew they had a dead body, although Ian was trying to be helpful saying, couldn't they just say he had made an emergency landing and then died. Alan was not so sure, hence he called Bill for advice. The advice that he handed out was simply inspired. Take the body back to your house and get Ian to say it's you. That way the debt you owe the old man is sorted.

"I checked my wife wasn't at home, she was I guess, with her lover so wouldn't be around. I knew she'd never planned to see me dead. It was a brilliant idea. Ian and I took the body back to my house, laid him out in the workshop and I left in Ian's car, letting him call the ambulance and make the identification.

"I went back to the airfield and picked up the parcel that still needed to be delivered. But it wasn't going to the old man, this one was for me. I called him to say the pilot had not turned up as expected, he said he would check the other end.

"With a big smile on my face, I went off to see Sylvia. If you didn't know she's my bit on the side. Me and the parcel of drugs which should be worth a few quid to keep me going, I could start a new life and my old lady could have her boss to herself. It seemed to work on every level."

"But then your body flies out of the coffin and things get complicated," Martin pointed out. He was intrigued as to why Alan was there in front of the two of them giving a full confession.

"Yes, but that wasn't the only fly in the ointment. In fact, if that was the only thing to have gone wrong, I wouldn't be sitting here today talking to the two of you.

"When I get to Sylvia's, she is confused, thinking when I said I was dead, I really was. But Sylvia is a little touched that way, although good in bed. Anyway, I open the parcel, I imagined some cocaine, a kilo, maybe two or three, at least worth enough to keep me going for a while.

"Not a trace of drugs, just three watches. That was all, three wrist watches, all telling the same time, well, an hour ahead, so I guessed they had come from Europe. What would I do with three watches?"

Putting his beer down, Alan moved towards the small flat screen TV that sat quietly in one alcove. He opened an insignificant drawer then pulled out three watches, which he dumped in Martin's hand.

"They're worth a few bob, I'll admit, but getting a good price for them, well, you'd have to know someone who's in that sort of trade very well. Limited market for those brands. It would have been so much easier with a kilo of cocaine."

Susan noticed Martin's eyes almost popping out of his head as he screamed, "Jesus, it can't be a Patek Philippe Nautilus. Are these real?"

"I guess so."

"It's a watch, Martin," Susan helpfully pointed out, as Martin fussed around putting the watch on his wrist, then admiring it from every angle.

"No Susan, this is not a watch. Any Patek Philippe watch is a work of art combined with pure Swiss craftsmanship. Just look at the way it caresses my wrist."

"If you're so in love with that watch, how come you've never bought one?"

Alan answered for Martin, he had already researched the three watches he had acquired illicitly. "A hundred and fifty grand."

"Sorry, do you actually mean one hundred and fifty thousand pounds, or just one hundred and fifty pounds."

"Yep," Alan confirmed. "One hundred and fifty thousand pounds for a watch."

"Not just any watch," Martin defended the treasure on his wrist. "Absolute craftsmanship, there's no better watch in the world."

"Martin," Susan wanted to bring him back to reality as he seemed to have become hypnotised, "it's a watch. It tells the time; you can't reverse time or go time-travelling with it. It just tells you how close you are to your next meal or when it's time for bed. I have a seven-pound watch from Asda which tells the time just the same as that Patek thing."

Martin took off the watch laying it carefully beside him on the fabric seat. He then picked up the next one that Alan had given him.

"Rolex Daytona?" Martin apprehensively asked, Alan nodded. "This one's more affordable but they still don't sell it at Asda. As I recall, this is worth maybe about forty thousand pounds."

"Martin, that's mad, I could buy a car for that, and it'd have a clock in it as well." Susan was surprised that any watch could be so expensive. But since she had started working with Martin, a lot of things had surprised her.

Alan added to her confusion when he contributed his own recently acquired knowledge of high value watches.

"Not that Daytona, that's a special edition. Something about its bracelet and watch face, it was too technical for me, but it'll fetch about one hundred and ten thousand on the second-hand market. The third one is a Vacheron. They're real diamonds on the clock face, one hundred and eighty thousand pounds. Three of them add up to a lot of money, but as I said, where would I sell them?"

"Let's get this right," Susan said, "those three watches are worth more than this whole caravan site, in fact you could buy most of Leysdown and still have change." She shook her head in disbelief.

"That's why it seems like the best thing is to give myself up, take the rap for what I've done and get on with my life. Why anyone wants to sneak watches into the country I have no idea, but old man Max appears to for some reason. I guess I'll have to give them back."

"The same reason anyone takes risks: the lure of money." She could see exactly why Max was quietly importing watches into the country. "If Max had those go through the normal channels, he'd need to pay VAT on them. Twenty per cent of, let's call it four hundred thousand pounds, is eighty thousand pounds. Plus, I bet he puts VAT on them when he sells. There's money to be made. "No drugs, just a tax fraud."

Martin carefully unclipped the Rolex Daytona and replaced it with his own watch, which now could be considered very cheap.

After he had put the watches safely back in the drawer under the TV, Alan continued with his story. Having realised that he was not going to have much money to start a new life, he had to find another way.

He approached his wife. They met up in Tesco and Alan offered her the option of him remaining dead. He told her she could have an automatic divorce in a couple of years and in the meantime, she could move in with her lover, Manny. His only condition was he needed one hundred thousand pounds in cash. It was a smaller part of the house value of which he would be entitled to half if he resurrected himself and then they divorced.

She agreed a little too eagerly, Alan thought, but obtaining that sort of money in cash was proving difficult. When he saw Martin and Susan knocking at his door, he felt the game was up and it was time to come back from the dead.

"What could they do me for? Helping out a tax fraudster, not reporting a dead French man and faking my own death. I'm sure if I help the prosecution case with nailing Max, I'll get a lighter sentence, maybe even a suspended one. Are you taking me in?"

"We could give you a lift to the police station if you want, but it would be better if you popped along to the local constabulary and told them the whole story," Martin suggested, not wanting to be tied up with bringing in a fugitive, that would no doubt only delay their Verona holiday. At least at this rate they looked on target to make the plane in a couple of days.

"Alan, I've an idea that might help you. Let me explain," Susan said. Something that always worried Martin, her ideas were not always helpful.

Chapter 26

The traffic was light as Martin drove away from Leysdown. He was in no rush to get to Max Phillip's house as he listened to Susan and her idea, although he was struggling to understand her reasoning.

She had several concerns with what Alan had told them. She concluded that his account of the situation was a concoction of fact and fantasy, with more than one or two inconsistencies in his story. Susan had picked up that he described the pilot as someone speaking a foreign language, saying he was not sure where the plane came from. Then at the end, he mentioned a dead French pilot.

A greater worry for Susan was that Alan seemed to imply that both Bill and he were responsible for the missing package, as in together they set about raising the cash to pay back Max Phillips. Yet, according to what he had said about the telephone call to Bill the night the French pilot died, Bill is alleged to have said that if he dies then the debt disappears. But Susan could not see it that way, Max would certainly still come after Bill for the compensation.

She also recalled that when they spoke to Bill Latham, he appeared to suggest that it was Alan who dealt with the plane landing and moving the parcel.

Plus, didn't Alan say that Bill hated Turkish cuisine? He implied that Bill didn't want to go to that restaurant. Susan impressed Martin when she recalled that she had seen the remains of a takeaway Turkish meal in Bill's kitchen. Why would Alan lie about such a thing? Because if the import scam was in full swing before he joined, then Bill would have had to go to the restaurant himself.

Alan was not telling the truth, Susan was convinced. Then what was it and how could they uncover it? It was her strategy that really concerned Martin.

"Why would Max Phillips want to tell us the truth?" Martin asked, worried that what she planned was risky.

"Because we now have something he wants."

That was true, Martin thought. Although it had come as a total surprise to him when Susan asked Alan if they could take the watches back to Max Phillips. He was understandably hesitating at first, until Susan explained that as far as most people were concerned, he tried to fake his own death. Why? To escape a loveless marriage and live with his true love, Sylvia. The importing side of his life was only known by a select few, most of whom would prefer all those shenanigans to be kept secret. Martin was not convinced, but he could understand her logic.

"Max either tells us the truth, or the watches end up in the hands of the police."

"But explain to me, my dear contriving wife, how will we know if Max is telling the truth? If we give him the watches back and keep quiet about the import business side of his life, aren't we, in the eyes of the law, just as guilty?"

"Possibly, but there's something else my woman's intuition is telling me that I can't share with you without breaking my solemn oath to womanhood. Just remember, as soon as we park at Mr Phillips's house, you take that Patek watch off and give it to me. So you'd better make the most of it for now."

Martin looked at the hugely expensive watch that temporarily adorned his wrist, he was in no rush to get to Max Phillips.

***

Max was wearing his traditional striped blazer. Today's colours were simple thin bands of blue and white. This co-ordinated with his light blue casual trousers and the blue ring around his fedora, which he wore even as he sat at his desk.

"Now that's a new one. Private investigators requiring the help of an old man like me. I presume this is to do with Alan?"

"It is, but it's as much to do with you as well," Susan smiled as she spoke. Martin decided it would be safer and easier just to sit and listen as she continued. "We know you're importing under the cover of darkness valuable merchandise, avoiding import duties as well as VAT. Now we know, as well as you do, that avoiding VAT is a crime."

Susan took from her pocket the three watches that Alan had handed over to her. With reverence she laid each one carefully in front of Max, allowing him the time to understand what they had in their custody.

"I guess these are the items that Alan had of yours, when he seemingly died. You can have them back on one condition. You tell us the whole truth and nothing less than the whole truth. If you do, you can have those back.

"But before you start, remember that we do have some undisputed facts, which if they don't fit in with what you're about to tell us, then everything will change. These watches end up in the hands of the police and you'll be looking at a jail sentence. Of course, if you do give us the truth, then the watches are yours and we have nothing to give to the police. The choice is yours, and yours alone."

Max looked down at the watches, they were certainly the ones that went astray the night that Alan proclaimed himself dead. Then he looked into Susan's eyes. She had attractive grey-green eyes, which gave nothing away. He thought that she would make a good poker player. The game she was proposing would be high in stakes.

"Why should I trust you, young lady? What's to stop you from hearing the whole story and then telling the authorities?"

"Because, Mr Phillips, at Lingfield you should have trusted me on the two-thirty-five race. I won a lot more than you. You need to trust my judgement."

Max picked up the Patek watch, rolled it between his fingers, and smiled.

"It's a beautiful watch you must admit." He paused considering his options, fewer in number than he would have liked. "If I give you the truth, you will drop any further investigation, I get these wonderful watches back and it will be as if we'd never met?"

"You have my word, but only if you give us the whole truth. We want to know everything about your relationship with Alan and his companions. You do that, then we won't pursue you any further."

The tense silence in the room filled the space like sand in a seaside bucket, packed down and ready to transform into a sandcastle.

"Alright, sit back and I'll tell you all."

For many years, he had imported not just expensive watches, but any sort of valuable artefact. Paintings, sculptures, jewellery, any small worthwhile antiques were included. If there was a profit in it for him, he was happy to act as a go-between. He described himself as a sort of transport manager bringing together seller and buyer.

Transporting such goods into the country via the established channels, often made him liable for import duties, complex paperwork and the dreaded VAT, adding a greater expense. While not too painful to his profit, it did curtail him from making a much larger return on the items he traded.

Once he had become well known in the trade, it was suggested to him that there were several buyers and sellers who would prefer that their transaction had no paper trail or formal record. Discretion was their objective.

Max veered his business towards these risky transactions, which were more lucrative. He liked the increase in profit but was aware smuggling through normal ports and transit hubs meant there was the ever-present risk of being caught.

It was suggested by a French dealer that if he could find a different secure route into the United Kingdom, then there would be bigger profits to be had.

"By chance during a conversation, a friend mentioned the protest at Pott's Field, which stopped the expansion of the airport, preventing night flights. I wondered about the possibility of having a plane land under the cover of darkness. My French counterpart agreed it would be a useful route in.

"Fate has a funny way of working. Alan had fitted my air conditioning system and had at the time mentioned he was giving up and going to work at Pott's Field. I knew he was happy to be bribed, as he had done all the work here for half the price as long as I paid cash, which I did. I would imagine his firm lost a lot of air conditioning equipment that weekend."

Max put it to Alan that if he facilitated the landing of a plane at night, then received and delivered a parcel to him, all without asking any questions, his reward would be significant. Alan was greedy, anything to make an easy penny, so he was more than happy to help. The arrangement was for him to be paid one thousand pounds each week, deliveries, or no deliveries. To avoid any direct traceable contact, he was paid in cash. Along with that payment, he would be given a list of any expected deliveries during the following seven days. It was usually just once a week but at times there had been as many as three.

It surprised Max just how much demand there was for this very discreet service. Although some of the transactions, for which he acted as an intermediary, were legitimate, they were still avoiding import duties. There were, he was sure, other commerce which included the movement of stolen goods, but he was not concerned, as long as he made a sizeable profit on each deal, he was happy. He was just the transport manager.

"To be clear," Susan interrupted, "Alan was your man at the airfield, he and he alone was the person you dealt with."

"Yes. The less people involved the better, that's the way illegal operations work. I do believe that Alan had a person at the airport who helped him with the night-time landings, but that was his concern. I presume he passed on a bit of what I was paying him."

The difficulty arose, Max admitted, when Alan foolishly lost the package containing some very attractive Louis XVI jewellery that he was due to deliver when his bike was stolen. Max ended up having to compensate the seller, so sought to recoup his losses from Alan. As he was providing such a beneficial service, Max was being very flexible with regard to repayment, yet he was firm that Alan would need to pay eventually.

"Then, as you know, Alan called me one night, close to midnight, to say that the plane hadn't arrived. Well, such things are not impossible, problems at the other end of the channel, weather, there are many factors that can impact on what we do.

"I called my contact in France who assured me the plane and the cargo had left on time. But after that I couldn't communicate with Alan. I was very suspicious and concerned. My first thought was that he'd run off with the package, which in the end it would seem he did, but at the time I wasn't sure. Then my man Archibald found out that Alan had died. Sad as I was, I was still missing a parcel of watches, as you now know. But things happen that you have no control over. I now needed to find a replacement for Alan."

Max smiled as he recalled the first visit they made, telling him that Alan could well be alive. At least there was hope for the parcel, which was his main concern.

He sent Archibald first to Ian, who seemed to know nothing, then to Sylvia who also had no information.

"Thankfully, I did have faith in the two of you and it would seem you have come up trumps. My losses have been reduced. For that I am very grateful. It was our day at the races that especially cemented the fact that you knew plenty about Alan. To be honest, Susan, when you told me that Alan had something of mine, I was very pleased indeed. I felt sure we could come to a mutually acceptable arrangement."

Susan smiled, that sounded very much like the truth. Alan was the main person all along, Ian and Bill were innocent bystanders who were happy to help for a few extra pounds. The whole conspiracy was coming together. Alan was not a nice man; Susan was now sure of that. Ever since she heard that Alan had left his so-called best friend to misidentify the body, then not pay him, all of that spoke volumes about Alan as a person.

There was just one bit that Susan needed to confirm. But she could not do that here, she needed to speak to someone else.

"Have I satisfied you? That's the truth, unfettered, without any omissions."

"You know what, Max, I do believe everything you've said. I always thought you were a dodgy person, but I also believed you were an honourable one. Old school villain, as my dad used to say."

"So, your investigation ends here?" Max sounded tentative and a little nervous.

"You have my word, Max, we won't be talking to the powers that be about your little business arrangement. You can have your watches back.

"There's just one thing, the day at the races, your friend Tony who wanted to join us, did you get to see him?"

"No, but we rarely speak anyway. However, I did call him that day to see what he wanted. It was nothing important. Apparently, he'd seen me at the racecourse and no doubt wanted a free ticket into the owners' enclosure."

Chapter 27

"I'm sorry Susan, I have to say it, we are not doing the right thing. We cannot and should not just turn a blind eye to what Max Phillips is doing. We're being as criminal as he is."

"All I'm going to say is that you need to trust me on this one. Have I ever let you down?"

Not sure how best to answer that question, Martin played safe and did not reply. He thought that would be for the best in the long run.

They followed Artemis into the living room which had not changed, except for a tray that was beside his chair. It contained the remains of his recent meal: an empty plate, a knife and fork and a half empty cup of tea.

As he sat down, his mood was sombre and cold. They sat in silence, before he gruffly asked, "Well?"

"We thought you might be pleased to hear that we've located and spoken face to face with Alan."

Artemis shrugged his shoulders. "I'd only be really interested if he was dead, then my insurance company would be paying out on his life policy. As I told you before, this should have been handed over to the police."

"I've been wondering," Susan quizzed him, "why did you decide to ask Hayden Investigations to look into Alan's disappearance?"

"I told you at the outset. I was anxious that the widow might be left in limbo without having the body of her husband. Then, there was the outside chance she was involved with him in a conspiracy to defraud my company."

"But why us? I understand that you and your company often use outside investigators, but they're generally big organisations, with big reputations. We're the opposite."

"You were recommended by colleagues in Grantham. I've told you all this."

Susan knew full well. She recalled the conversation they had at the Papillon restaurant and how excited she was to take on the case, being treated like a real detective. Sadly, she had learnt that might not have been the whole truth behind his request.

"You see, I have it on good authority that the only reason you decided to employ Hayden Investigations to pursue the case of the missing body, was you believed we were incompetent."

"You're mistaken."

"No, I'm not," Susan was definitive in her words. She knew everything and wanted to lead Artemis down a track where he could not turn around.

"The case of Alan Hall was an everyday task for you. All you needed was confirmation that he was either dead or alive, you weren't bothered either way. That was until you saw his mobile phone records and the very last call he made just before his disappearance. A short call to Max Phillips changed everything for you."

"Why should it?"

"Because Max Phillips, or to use his correct name, Maximus Marc Anthony Phillips, is your stepbrother."

Now at this point of the conversation, Martin was thinking he should begin to take notes, for no better reason than he was losing the plot entirely. It was bad enough Susan saying Hayden Investigations were incompetent, that was cruel, maybe close to the truth but not a nice thing for her to say out loud. Now, Max and Artemis stepbrothers? How did Susan even arrive at that conclusion? Although he was more than a little bewildered, Martin remained quiet.

"Really," Artemis sounded less confident than he had. He waited to hear more from Susan, who was happy to continue.

"Yes. The very first time I met you, you introduced yourself as Artemis Anthony Ellison. Okay, long name, but everyone has their cross to bear. Then, as I've mentioned, investigating Max Phillips should easily have been in your remit. But you decided to keep your distance, employ an outside contractor. You didn't want to personally investigate the activities of your stepbrother.

"While I was at the races with Max, a Tony wanted to speak to him, a Tony, who Max said he rarely spoke to. You hate horse racing, but you needed to talk to your stepbrother and thought that would be a good opportunity. Maybe warn him that detectives were looking into his nocturnal activities.

"Then you said you saw Max and his manservant at the races. How did you even know Max had a manservant? The fact is, the closer we got to what Max was doing, the more nervous you were becoming.

"Max told me about his mother who'd divorced and remarried. It's strange what people tell you between races after a few drinks. His mother had two more children: a girl called Carol and a younger boy called Tony. He told me about Carol marrying some high-flying stockbroker, and his stepbrother, who he had heard was divorced, worked in insurance. Obviously, he thought selling insurance, not investigating claims.

"But why employ an incompetent pair of detectives? Maybe you had an inkling of what Max was up to in his business. Maybe you wanted to let us screw up the whole investigation and then all the correct boxes would be ticked, and no one could ever accuse you of turning a blind eye to your stepbrother's illegal activities."

The grin on Artemis's face was the broadest that they had ever seen. He seemed to be either happy or relieved.

"You know that before I engaged the Hayden team, although I had heard good things about you from my colleagues in Grantham, I thought from my own assessments, you were hapless and hopeless. You have proved me to be totally wrong; you're in fact a very shrewd duo."

Martin was pleased to accept such praise, not that he was sure how much of the glory he could claim.

"Yes, Maximus is my stepbrother, who my mother appeared to adore more than me even though she was divorced from his father. She regularly visited him and told me his name was from the Latin 'the greatest', whereas mine is a Greek female god, although she was goddess of the hunt among other things. Maybe that was what drew me to insurance investigations.

"You're exactly right. When I saw Max's number on Alan's call list, I knew that it would be difficult for me to pursue him. I might not have that much contact with him, but he was still family; I'd always protect him for my mother's sake. Anything I did might be construed as favouritism. Especially as I was aware that most of his business transactions were in the grey area of trading, I didn't want to harm those activities.

"Hayden Investigations seemed the perfect partner. A below average agency, which would shake a few branches but was unlikely to get to the heart of the matter. I was mistaken in that respect.

"You say you have now spoken to Alan."

Without any further reference to the family connection, Susan began to share with him all they had learnt from Alan, which was in many parts at odds with the other witnesses they had spoken to. It was Max, who provided the nearest thing to a genuine timeline of the events that led up to Alan's disappearance.

"But if you've said to Max, or promised, you would not investigate or take things further, not that I am complaining, I wanted to avoid any chance that he might be found out. But isn't that against the code that investigators have?" Artemis asked, wondering why they had given such an undertaking.

Martin, as quiet as he had been, wanted to ask that same question. In fact, he had been trying to get an answer to his concerns for most of the day. Whichever way he looked at it, Max Phillips was breaking the law. He had a henchman who roughed up Ian Cook in the hope of getting information. Max was not nice. He was a criminal and

Hayden Investigations had the proof. So why was Susan keen to turn a blind eye, maybe she would tell Artemis.

"I guess it is," Susan admitted. "But we aren't taking it any further, you will be contacting the police. See, I wasn't exactly lying to Max, more not telling the whole truth."

"Why would I take it any further? You've already discovered that he's part of my family. Also, you know that I wasn't keen to continue an investigation that might inhibit his business arrangements."

This was going to be the most difficult part for Susan, why would he, and how would she convince him? Overall, she thought she was a good judge of character, as a woman she needed to be. Often, she had been approached at a bar or in a club by a man she might never have seen before. He'd start talking to her. She knew that the purpose of his conversation was not about collecting her views on politics or the economic situation of the country. It was about getting friendly and starting a relationship that might last for the next few hours, the next few weeks or even longer. Susan had learnt to filter out the men who were shady, untrustworthy, lecherous, or just plain ugly and stupid. This enabled her to interact with a man who was generally acceptable to her standard and fitted into her emotional status at the time.

Usually, she was bad at choosing men for long term relationships, but short term, or at least separating the chaff from the wheat, she was, if she said so herself, pretty good.

Ever since she had met Artemis, she felt he was a kind man, someone who would fight for the underdog. His dress sense was questionable like his stepbrother's, obviously a family trait. But that was not important at the present time, it was his decency that she was relying on.

"You might love your stepbrother, but what he's doing is wrong and I think you know that. You'd be the last person to want to collect the evidence of what he's doing. All along he was just your stepbrother doing some shady deals, well, why not, what harm was it doing?

"Then we come along and tell you that your sweet Maximus is defrauding the revenue services of possibly a million pounds a year. That's a lot of lost tax, tax which pays for things like hospitals, schools, supports poor families. One million pounds, not available to those in need. That's what your stepbrother's shady dealings are actually doing. He is depriving a hospital somewhere of forty nurses. Forty nurses who could save how many lives, I wouldn't like to think.

"Looking at it that way, his shady dealings are as bad committing murder or at the very least manslaughter.

"He has to be stopped, for the sake of those people who need a nurse to help them live. We have the evidence. You need to present it through your company to the authorities."

"Murder, that's a big crime! Maybe Max isn't fulfilling his tax liabilities in full, but murder, I think you're being over-dramatic."

"No, I'm not," Susan sounded angry. "Hospitals are paid for by taxpayers, the likes of you and me, we pay for it, not the government. It's our money they're using. So, when your smart Max decides he isn't going to pay his taxes, then as I said, forty nurses aren't around to help people who are suffering ill health. Those lack of resources in the health service result in deaths, deaths which needn't have happened if your stepbrother paid his proper taxes. He might not be sticking a knife in someone, but he is just as responsible for their death. Murder is the word I'm sticking to. I think you of all people should understand."

There was a silence, a heavy one that Susan was happy to wait out. She was not going to say another word until Artemis spoke. She looked at him, there was a thoughtful look in his eye. Susan knew the story of how Emily died, she'd read a short newspaper report. She just wanted to hear it from Artemis.

He was now staring intently at the small photograph frame beside him, the young girl in it smiling, laughing. He picked it up, held it close to him, then spoke without looking at the others in the room. He appeared to be communicating to the young girl in the photograph who was his daughter. Then he presented it for them to see.

"I've told you this is Emily, my young daughter. She was just six when this picture was taken. Then about two weeks later she came off her bike, like every young child does when they're learning to ride. My wife and I thought she had lost consciousness for a minute or two. We called an ambulance. They arrived and took her and us to the local A&E, where we sat for over an hour. Emily was chatting away at first, then she seemed to become confused. She was pushed to the head of the queue. The doctors examined her and decided that she needed critical care. There was a possible bleed on the brain.

"We were at Queen Mary's in Sidcup, where all the intensive care beds had been filled. There was no space for my Emily. They got an ambulance and arranged to send her to St Thomas's Hospital in central London. Even with blue lights and sirens, with your young daughter beside you suffering, it seemed a long journey. When we thankfully arrived, she was unconscious.

"Only to be told the one bed they had spare, the one bed that was there when Queen Mary's had told them about Emily, my Emily, was now occupied by a seriously injured cyclist who had been struck by a lorry.

"Emily still needed critical care and that care was becoming more and more vital. They found her a bed, an intensive care bed. Where do you think?"

The question was obviously rhetorical, they remained silent.

"They took my daughter to Cambridge. Bloody Addenbrooke's Cambridge, sixty miles from St Thomas's in London. They had a bed, in fact they had two high-dependency beds. The ambulance drove fast, lights and sirens parting the traffic.

"My daughter died just before the Birchanger Green Services, she passed away on the M11 motorway. That's not a place anyone should die, let alone a six-year-old child."

The silence fell like a curtain between the three of them. Artemis felt an emptiness that started to fill with sad emotions and painful memories.

"You're right, she died because of a lack of resources. Queen Mary's didn't have enough beds. My local hospital, who could have saved her, didn't have enough beds.

"You're right, people like Max need to be stopped. His is not a victimless crime, he contributed to Emily's death. He needs to be stopped for the sake of others. I'll make a call to my office. We'll alert the police to his activities."

Susan wanted to smile, but felt the mood of the room, now was not the moment to rejoice. Instead, she went over to Artemis and hugged him, she had seen the tears welling in his eyes.

The emotional atmosphere was broken into when Martin's phone rang, he quickly answered it.

"Arrested? What are you talking about Colin?"

Artemis and Susan turned trying to listen to his conversation.

"Okay, I'll tell them."

"Tell us what?" Susan asked, her arm still around Artemis's shoulder.

"The police have arrested Alan and Max. As well as taking Ian and Bill in for questioning. It would seem the authorities have already found out."

Chapter 28

Yesterday had been a busy day and Martin was exhausted. He might have lain in bed a lot longer had he not heard the back door creak open. He looked at his watch, ten past seven. Sam and Kenny were arriving. He rolled over, Susan was snoring and blissfully unaware that the house was being overrun by kitchen constructors.

Wrapped in his dressing gown, Martin walked downstairs and into the kitchen where Kenny was busy taking out bits of kitchen cupboards and Sam was under the sink doing something technical no doubt.

"We did as you asked," Martin confirmed. "The fridge freezer is now in the dining room, along with the microwave and the kettle."

From under the sink Sam called out, "Great, I'll leave the water running, the sink will be gone but you'll have a tap here."

"Just no dishwasher," Martin pointed out.

"Well as I told your missus," his voice muffled by the surroundings, "it's complex doing a kitchen. If we can clear it all out in one go, then we can get the new one in quicker, and it'll be cheaper." He appeared from his hide under the sink clutching two oddly shaped white plastic pipes, one of which Martin had seen before, but was still unsure of its purpose.

"Well, we're off on our break the day after tomorrow, so you will have the whole place to yourselves. I trust you'll be finished by the time we get back?"

"You have my word; you'll arrive back to a smashing new kitchen."

Martin cautiously stepped over the debris and tools so he could fill the kettle before retiring to the relative safety of the living room, now a makeshift kitchen. He offered the workmen a drink which they readily accepted.

Kenny, tea with lots of milk and no sugar, Sam, Martin recalled, was milk and three sugars. They all stood with their teas in the kitchen admiring, if that was the correct expression, the emptiness of the room now Kenny had jettisoned the last wooden frame into the skip.

"Nice place you got here," Sam observed, "must have cost a pretty penny. Detecting trade on the up?"

"Sadly, there does seem to be a lot of detecting to do nowadays." Martin heard his voice echo off the bare walls. "But you guys don't do so bad do you?"

"We earn a living. Hard work mind, look forward to my weekend off; give the muscles a rest."

"Well, I see you have a brand-new van outside, not even sign-written yet?"

Martin had noticed the shiny van parked on the drive, a plain white van looking showroom new, without so much as a scratch on it. Unlike their other van, battered and bruised, with the driver's side looking as if it had scraped along a crash barrier.

"Little bit of work needed on it, so I've hired the one outside."

By this time Kenny had gulped almost half his piping hot tea in one swallow, the second mouthful emptied the mug. He pulled out a sandwich from a Tupperware box he had brought with him, then laughed.

"Bit of work! You're having a laugh Sam. You almost wrecked the whole thing." Kenny looked at Martin, grinning broadly with a crust of white bread still hanging from his mouth. Martin was not sure of the contents, but the sandwich filling looked to be a mixture of mashed potato, cabbage, onion and brown sauce. Kenny continued, "He hit a bleedin' hearse trying to film it while speeding along the road. You must have heard about it, the one with the bouncing body. Getting six points on yer licence for it, ain't you, Sammy boy."

"Kenny!" Sam recalled explaining to his mate earlier, that although they had had a good laugh about it in the café with others, mentioning it in this house was taboo. "Didn't we have a discussion about this?"

"It was you that hit the hearse?"

Sam could see no point in denying the fact, given that Kenny had already admitted it loud and clear.

"Shamed to say it was me. Just didn't think it in our best interest to mention it around you, given you were doing the investigation and stuff."

"It depends how you look at it." Martin laughed. "On the one hand, you gave me work which I do try my best to avoid. But looking on the bright side, according to my wife, your careless driving has exposed a tax fraud. The result of that unfortunate accident has helped save a number of lives. Don't ask me to explain. Just accept we never really know what our actions, good or bad, might result in. More tea?"

Chapter 29

"This isn't your car, is it?" Martin asked as Colin levered the last of the suitcases into the boot of the silver Mercedes.

"God no, my pension doesn't stretch to limousines. But as a good friend, I thought I'd splash out while taking you and the missus to the airport. Is that all the cases?"

"I think so, but until my wife appears at the door, I wouldn't like to guarantee we're fully loaded."

Both men waited beside the car. Dawn was just breaking with a damp chill in the air, the grass laden with dew.

It was because of the early start that Colin stayed the night before; it was the least they could do after taking up his generous offer to drive them to Gatwick Airport. In hindsight, the arrangement was not the best plan. They spent the evening eating a Chinese takeaway, and drinking before drinking some more while Colin enlightened them with the current situation Max and Alan now found themselves in. On several occasions during the evening, they toasted themselves to a job well done, which was not strictly true. There was an unplanned intervention which had brought the case to a satisfactory conclusion.

Although Colin, Martin and Susan were taking credit for the arrest and subsequent charges brought against Alan and Max, there was another person involved, Jason Bennett.

He was a teenager, who was known locally as a troublemaker. Having just turned seventeen, the gaunt youth was living off the crumbs of society, or at least anything he could thieve and sell. He was well-known to the police, with a list of petty crimes that Fagin would have been proud of if Jason had been part of his squad.

Technically he lived at home with his father, mother and two sisters. In reality, it was a place he tried to avoid at all costs. His father was doing three years for assault, resulting in a household with three squabbling females, which as Jason told his best mate, 'Does me head in.'

Living most of his life on the streets, he was always looking for distractions and opportunities. Such an opportunity presented itself late one night as he walked past a petrol station. Alongside a pump there was a newly filled Yamaha motorbike, which even had the keys in the ignition. Well, Jason thought, if someone is that stupid, they need to be taught a lesson.

Swiftly and without hesitation, he flipped his hood over his head, strode on to the forecourt, sat astride the bike, started it, and drove away. It took no more than twenty seconds. He was aware as he drove out onto the road of a man screaming and shouting behind him. Serves you right, he thought.

From experience, Jason knew that he might have a couple of hours riding around and having fun with the bike before it would be wise to dump it. The police would soon have the bike listed as being stolen and he was not in the mood to lead the police around on a chase through the back streets of the estate. Just after midnight having driven the bike through fields, some roads, raced along footpaths and done wheelies in Morrison's car park, he decided it was time to dump his latest toy and move on.

There was a locked trunk box on the back of the bike which soon burst open with the screwdriver Jason always carried with him, handy for so many things. It was a bit like Christmas, not that he had ever had many presents during the season of giving, his family were not givers, more takers. But any locked box was exciting, you never knew what you might find. He rummaged through it.

There were a range of tools neatly wrapped in cloth, some Allen keys, a wrench, a flat-head screwdriver, a handful of cable ties, a roll of duct tape, as well as a set of battery cables. Also, the owner was no doubt someone who liked to be prepared for anything, as there was a puncture repair kit and a CO_2 canister to pump up a flat tyre. Nothing so far of much value.

In addition, there was a package, a cereal-sized box wrapped in brown paper and heavily taped. Jason made use of the tools to break open the pack which revealed a box, that in turn was filled with bubble wrap. In the very centre, wrapped in tissue paper, Jason found a brooch.

It was a colourful brooch with red and green jewels, also some clear sparkling stones which he guessed could be diamonds, but more than likely were the fake sort that everyone buys nowadays. It was ugly, butt ugly, Jason thought, but he was not going to keep it. It would be sold. He might get thirty quid for it if he was lucky. That would see him alright in pie and chips for the next few nights. He stuffed it into his pocket, kicked the bike over and walked off. Maybe he would go home, hopefully the women would all be either asleep or drunk, if so, he might get a few hours kip. Nicking and driving around aimlessly was tiring work.

From time to time, he recalled that he had a trinket in his pocket that he could flog, then he would get distracted, it would go out of his mind. At the weekend, he went out with his mates. After having a few beers, while walking home he fell down an embankment covering himself and his clothes in brown sticky mud. The jeans were left on the floor of his bedroom. Couldn't go nicking in dirty jeans, that was not the way to dress for work.

In the Bennett household, the washing machine had little to do. It was for most of the inhabitants of the house a bit of a pain to sort the washing out and get it done. It was only used occasionally. The sisters always believed it was easier to go out and nick clothes from a shop, then throw them out once they got dirty. That got rid of any evidence of their shoplifting, shrewd they thought.

This lack of laundry was fortunate for Jason as it was a good few weeks later that he recalled the trinket he had found. He retrieved it from his jeans which were caked in dried soil.

He took it to his favourite pawn brokers and offered it up for valuation. Seeing it in the daylight, he wondered if it might be worth about fifty, which would be handy as he was planning to take a girl out at the weekend and could impress her with a slap-up meal at a surviving Wimpy Bar.

The pawnbroker, Mr Tideway, was an expert on antique jewellery, which for Jason was the worst thing that could have happened.

Colin continued the story for his hosts as he filled his glass.

"Mr Tideway asks the little tearaway, 'Where did you get this?' Fair question to which Jason replies, 'It was my grandmother's. Gave it to me on her death bed, but I need the cash, life can be cruel'. Mr Tideway shook his head, well, he would, he knew Jason and knew his grandmother was not Marie Antoinette. He was confident that the brooch in front of him was from the time of Louis XVI.

"Tideway told little Jason that he knew it was nicked and was about to call the police. You didn't see Jason for dust," Colin laughed.

The police were very interested in what Mr Tideway had told them and agreed that such a valuable gem was outside of the normal remit of Jason Bennett. That was the reason they kept an eye out for him and interrupted a romantic meal he was having in a Wimpy Bar. They questioned him in the back of the police car.

It did not take long for Jason to tell them about the bike, why should he lie? With a bit of luck, they'd go and forget about his misdemeanour. They did go as did Jason's date.

"Now Suzie baby, your chat with Alan Hall obviously didn't work. He arrived home. Sat down with his wife to thrash out a new arrangement where she gets her plumber boyfriend, and he gets some cash in his hand. The reason he wanted the cash was to do a moonlight once again and disappear. He was still running from Max."

Colin grabbed a handful of salted peanuts and chomped them as he spoke, a glass of wine in his hand ready to wash them down.

"Christine was just pleased to get shot of him anyway she could, and looked forward to the day Manny, the plumber, was on hand to sort out her pipework, if you get my meaning.

"Having decided what suited everyone, they foolishly answered the door to three police officers who were pleased to say they had recovered the stolen bike. Alan thought all his Christmas's had come together. With the bike back, the package could be returned to Max Phillips. The debt hanging over him would be wiped out. He could be so naïve at times.

"They asked why he happened to have a Louis XVI brooch in his possession, it was worth a lot of money. Things were not going well for Alan, how do you explain such an item, a gift for the wife, the one you are about to leave for good. From that point on everything unravelled, even more so when one officer calmly pointed out that according to their records, Alan should be dead. They knew it all.

"Alan, Max, Archibald, Bill and Ian were all arrested. Which means you had kept your promise to Max, and dear sweet Artemis didn't have to grass up his relation. I think all in all a great conclusion for everyone."

They celebrated by opening a bottle of champagne. Martin had bought a pack of smoky bacon crisps especially for the occasion, knowing Colin's liking for them. They all dipped their crisps, following Colin's tradition, into their champagne and laughed.

***

At last Martin was on his way to starting a holiday with his wife. It had looked a distinct possibility that they would miss out on the break. Somehow, everything had worked out in the end and here he was in the back of the car with Susan alongside him, as Colin drove towards Gatwick airport. Colin had insisted on wearing a chauffeur's hat, which looked completely out of place against his make-up, bright red hair and houndstooth patterned jacket. But Colin is Colin, thought Martin.

"In all the excitement I forgot to ask," he turned to Susan, "what was it at Castle Farm Stables that ignited your interest in horse racing?"

Colin answered from the front, "Castle Farm? Suzie Baby, isn't that where you were rolling about in the hay and lost your cherry?"

"Colin!" She remonstrated, that was not how she would have put it, certainly not to Martin.

"How come he knew?"

"Girls talk."

"He's a bloke in women's clothing."

"That's close enough. Anyway, it's not important, but yes, I'll admit it was the place I lost my virginity to a young stable boy called..." she hesitated.

"Gavin," Colin contributed. "Don't worry Martin I wasn't there, it's just I've got a better memory than Suzie Baby."

"I presume Becky knows the story; in fact, I guess most of your friends know it."

"As I told you, us girls talk, plus I know I wasn't the first woman that you went to bed with. Who was it, Paula?"

"Not sure I can help you there," Colin called out, "but what I can tell you is, Martin's love of Shakespeare has its roots in the fact..."

"Colin, I thought we'd agreed..."

"I'm just balancing out the way I share knowledge. As I was saying Suzie Baby, Martin's love of Shakespeare can be put down to the breast size of his English teacher who he had a crush on. If he asks you to wear a mortar board and gown in bed, say no."

"I was a teenager." Martin felt the embarrassment of the revelation flush his cheeks.

"Okay, who was your first? I hope it wasn't your well-proportioned teacher."

Fortunately for Martin, as Susan asked the question they arrived at the terminal. He was able to put off his answer, promising her he would tell all when they got to the hotel over a romantic candlelit evening meal that he had planned. Although he was not sure such a subject was a suitable topic of conversation for it.

They thanked Colin, loaded their suitcases onto a trolley and made their way into the airport terminal, joining the shifting crowds as they sought the Verona express check-in desk. Martin hated queues.

Having checked in their luggage, clutching their boarding cards, Martin felt he was finally on his way to Verona. Holding Susan's hand, they made their way towards the security checks. He hated that part; it always made him feel guilty. He recalled an embarrassing experience at a French airport that Susan was happy to remind him of.

This time everything went to plan; they were now free to find a bar. Their holiday had now begun. As they chinked glasses, Martin's phone rang, he checked the caller information.

"Pinky Pead, I wonder what he wants?"

THE END

Author Notes

Well, it had to happen. After Martin decided on a genuine date with Susan, the result was clearly inevitable: marriage.

I'm sure some of you will be disappointed there was no wedding to read about, but let's be honest, would it really be fair to lumber them with an investigation during their honeymoon?

Now that they are married, there are still many cases that will crop up for them to unravel. There will also be those domestic situations which will bring a bit of disagreement, plus, as upstanding residents of Highfield, the locals will, no doubt, see the advantage of having two detectives in the village. More of that in the next book.

The idea for this story originated from my being overtaken by an undertaker's limousine – I know, it doesn't sound right to be overtaken by a limousine laden with a coffin on the M3 just outside Basingstoke. I wasn't going slowly, but he was going faster. My very abstract psyche wondered what would happen if by chance it collided with another vehicle and the wrong body was inside. Originally, I mapped the idea out as a thriller – I write those as well - but in the end Martin and Susan were given the investigation to handle, which they did in my opinion very well.

Please do let me know what you think about Mr & Mrs Hayden's latest escapade.

Until the next time.

Adrian

Acknowledgements

As ever, the process of getting this story onto your Kindle or into your hands as a paperback, takes more than just one person.

I wanted to give the local funeral directors credit for answering my often-stupid questions about their profession. They preferred not to be mentioned, understandably given the circumstances of the story. But thank you anyway.

As for the watchmaker, Patek Philippe, helpful as they were, apparently, they don't give out free samples! Hence, I'm sticking to my Skagen watch.

I also want to thank a good friend, who allowed me to highlight his obsession with trainers, questionable fashion sense and his caring nature. Artemis Ellison is very much based on him. Thank you for being a good sport.

However, the real hard work is done by Irene, Jean, Angela, Claire, Brian, Pete and Anthony, who all took the time and trouble to read through the story, offering up valuable advice as well as pointing out slip-ups. Thank you.

As I am writing this, my wife is bravely going through my next book, knocking it into shape, thankfully she is giggling, at the humour, I hope.

Books by Adrian Spalding

The Reluctant Detective

The Reluctant Detective Goes South

The Reluctant Detective Under Pressure

The Reluctant Detective Goes North

The Reluctant Detective Wants a Break

Sleeping Malice

Caught on Camera

The Night You Murder

Stay in touch for my latest news.

www.adrianspalding.co.uk

books@adrianspalding.co.uk

Join my Mailing list.

Facebook

Printed in Great Britain
by Amazon